KU-255-095

A Brave New Series

GLOBAL ISSUES
IN A CHANGING WORLD

This new series of short, accessible think-pieces deals with leading global issues of relevance to humanity today. Intended for the enquiring reader and social activists in the North and the South, as well as students, the books explain what is at stake and question conventional ideas and policies. Drawn from many different parts of the world, the series' authors pay particular attention to the needs and interests of ordinary people, whether living in the rich industrial or the developing countries. They all share a common objective – to help stimulate new thinking and social action in the opening years of the new century.

Global Issues in a Changing World is a joint initiative by Zed Books in collaboration with a number of partner publishers and non-governmental organizations around the world. By working together, we intend to maximize the relevance and availability of the books published in the series.

Participating NGOs

Both ENDS, Amsterdam
Catholic Institute for International Relations, London
Corner House, Sturminster Newton
Council on International and Public Affairs, New York
Dag Hammarskjöld Foundation, Uppsala
Development GAP, Washington DC
Focus on the Global South, Bangkok
Inter Pares, Ottawa
Public Interest Research Centre, Delhi
Third World Network, Penang
Third World Network–Africa, Accra
World Development Movement, London

About this Series

Communities in the South are facing great difficulties in coping with global trends. I hope this brave new series will throw much needed light on the issues ahead and help us choose the right options.

Martin Khor, Director, Third World Network, Penang

There is no more important campaign than our struggle to bring the global economy under democratic control. But the issues are fearsomely complex. This Global Issues series is a valuable resource for the committed campaigner and the educated citizen.

Barry Coates, Director, World Development Movement (WDM)

Zed Books has long provided an inspiring list about the issues that touch and change people's lives. The Global Issues series is another dimension of Zed's fine record, allowing access to a range of subjects and authors that, to my knowledge, very few publishers have tried. I strongly recommend these new, powerful titles and this exciting series.

John Pilger, author

We are all part of a generation that actually has the means to eliminate extreme poverty world-wide. Our task is to harness the forces of globalization for the benefit of working people, their families and their communities – that is our collective duty. The Global Issues series makes a powerful contribution to the global campaign for justice, sustainable and equitable development, and peaceful progress.

Glenys Kinnock MEP

About this Book

How to manage the world economy – and, more fundamentally, whether humanity wishes it to go in an ever more market-oriented, transnational corporation-dominated and capital-footloose direction – is the most important international question of our time. In this short and trenchant history of those bodies – the World Bank, IMF, WTO and Group of Seven – which have promoted this economic globalization, Walden Bello

- points to their manifest failings
- examines the major new ideas put forward for reforming the management of the world economy
- argues for a much more fundamental shift towards a decentralized, pluralistic system of global economic governance allowing countries to follow development strategies sensitive to their own values and particular mix of constraints and opportunities.

About the Author

Walden Bello is the founding director of Focus on the Global South, a policy research institute based in Bangkok, Thailand. Prior to that, he was executive director of the Institute for Food and Development Policy (Food First) in Oakland, California. Educated at Princeton University, where he did his doctorate in sociology in 1975, he subsequently taught at the University of California, Berkeley, where he was a research associate with the Center for South East Asian Studies. A renowned campaigner for international justice and development and one of the leading independent critics in the South of current global economic arrangements, he is the author of numerous books, including:

A Siamese Tragedy: Development and Disintegration in Modern Thailand (with Shea Cunningham and Li Kheng Poh) (1999)

Dark Victory: The United States, Structural Adjustment and Global Poverty (with Shea Cunningham) (1994)

People and Power in the Pacific: The Struggle for the Post-Cold War Order (1992)

Dragons in Distress: Asia's Miracle Economies in Crisis (with Stephanie Rosenfeld) (1991)

Brave New Third World? Strategies for Survival in the Global Economy (1990)

Development Debacle: The World Bank in the Philippines (1982)

Deglobalization: Ideas for a New World Economy

WALDEN BELLO

University Press Ltd
DHAKA

White Lotus Co. Ltd
BANGKOK

Fernwood Publishing Ltd
NOVA SCOTIA

Books for Change
BANGALORE

David Philip
CAPE TOWN

Zed Books
LONDON · NEW YORK

Deglobalization: Ideas for a New World Economy was first published in 2002 by:

in Bangladesh: The University Press Ltd, Red Crescent Building, 114 Motijheel C/A, PO Box 2611, Dhaka 1000

in Burma, Cambodia, Laos, Thailand and Vietnam: White Lotus Co. Ltd, GPO Box 1141, Bangkok 10501, Thailand

in Canada: Fernwood, 8422 St Margaret's Bay Road (Hwy 3), Site 2A, Box 5, Black Point, Nova Scotia B0J 1B0

in India: Books for Change, 139 Richmond Road, Bangalore 560 025

in Southern Africa: David Philip Publishers (Pty Ltd), 99 Garfield Road, Claremont 7700, South Africa

in the rest of the world: Zed Books Ltd, 7 Cynthia Street, London N1 9JF, UK and Room 400, 175 Fifth Avenue, New York, NY 10010, USA

www.zedbooks.demon.co.uk

Copyright © Walden Bello, 2002

The right of Walden Bello to be identified as the author of this work has been asserted by him in accordance with the Copyright, Designs and Patents Act, 1988

Cover designed by Andrew Corbett
Designed and set in Monotype Bembo and VAG Rounded by Ewan Smith, London
Printed and bound in the United Kingdom by Cox & Wyman, Reading

Distributed in the USA exclusively by Palgrave, a division of St Martin's Press, LLC, 175 Fifth Avenue, New York, NY 10010

All rights reserved

A catalogue record for this book is available from the British Library
US CIP data is available from the Library of Congress
Canadian CIP data is available from the National Library of Canada

ISBN 1 55266 099 0 pb (Canada)
ISBN 81 87380 73 X pb (India)
ISBN 0 86486 602 X pb (Southern Africa)
ISBN 1 84277 304 6 hb (Zed Books)
ISBN 1 84277 305 4 pb (Zed Books)

Contents

Acknowledgements and Dedication

Parts of this book originally appeared in a report prepared for the Commission on Globalization of the Parliament of the Federal Republic of Germany. I would like to thank Ulrich von Weizäcker, Elmar Altvater, Marianne Beisheim and the other members of the Commission and its staff for their encouragement and co-operation.

Robert Molteno of Zed was, as usual, extremely helpful in moving this project from conceptualization to publication, and I am very grateful for this.

My co-workers in Focus on the Global South and the Sociology Department of the University of the Philippines (UP) provided a very supportive context for this project, as did the Sociology Department and the Center for Southeast Asian Studies of the University of California at Los Angeles (UCLA), where the final stages of the writing took place. I wish to express my profound gratitude to these institutions and friends.

Most of the ideas expressed here emerged out of a collective enterprise, from a truly global movement in which I have had the extraordinary luck to participate. It is to all the fine people in this movement that I would like to dedicate this book. To be especially noted are colleagues, comrades and co-workers in the World Social Forum (WSF), Our World is not for Sale Coalition, the Asian Peace Alliance and the International Forum on Globalization (IFG).

Anuradha Mittal, Nicola Bullard, Marylou Malig, Robin Broad, John Cavanagh, Shalmali Guttal, Aileen Kwa, Debi Barker, Barbara Gaerlan, Angkarb Korsieporn, Jim Heddle, Marybeth Brangen,

Fred Zanoria, Tessie Zanoria, Mika Zanoria, Ike de la Cruz, Prosy de la Cruz, Suranuch Thongsila, Ami Ferrer, Patrick McGrath, Annette Ferrer, Allison Handler and Vernie Caparas supplied much-needed encouragement, inspiration and friendship at various points during the writing process.

Finally, I cannot thank my wife Maria Elena Abesamis enough for her unfailing support, friendship and companionship throughout.

Walden Bello
Los Angeles

ONE

Introduction: The Multiple Crises of Global Capitalism

This book is about the genesis and development of the current system of global economic governance and alternatives to it. It focuses on institutions that go under the rubric of multilateral institutions, specifically the G-8, the Bretton Woods institutions, and the World Trade Organization. While governance – a nice neutral word – is often described as the function of these institutions, a more appropriate description of their role might be maintenance of the hegemony of the system of global capitalism and promotion of the primacy of the states and economic interests that mainly benefit from it.

Around the mid-1990s, this system of global economic governance entered into crisis. The crisis of the multilateral institutions, however, is part of a bigger crisis of legitimacy that is affecting the system of global capitalism. The most obvious manifestation of this crisis was the growth of a powerful movement that confronted the representatives of the big powers, the big corporations and the multilateral organizations in city after city, meeting after meeting, the most historic being now known as the 'Battle of Seattle'. September 11 stopped the movement in its tracks, and many observers from the establishment confidently wrote it off as a significant global actor. As the massive assemblies in Barcelona in early March 2002 on the occasion of the European Union summit and in Porto Alegre a few weeks earlier at the World Social Forum (WSF) revealed, however, they were wrong.

It is the different dimensions of this broader crisis that are sketched out in this introduction. Specifically, we will look at six intersecting crises: those of multilateralism, the neoliberal vision and order, the corporation, the system of military hegemony, liberal democracy and the global production system.

From Triumph to Crisis

The last decade of the twentieth century began with the re-sounding collapse of the socialist economies of Eastern Europe and a lot of triumphalist talk about the genesis of a new market-driven global economy that rendered borders obsolete and rode on the advances of information technology. The key agents of the new global economy were the transnational corporations, depicted as the supreme incarnation of market freedom owing to their superior ability to bring about the most efficient mix of land, labour, capital and technology.

Halfway through the decade the World Trade Organization (WTO) was born. Partisans of globalization claimed it would provide the legal and institutional scaffolding for the new global economy. By creating a rules-based global system grounded in the primordial principle of free trade, the WTO would serve as the catalyst of an economic process that would bring about the greatest good for the greatest number. It was the third pillar of a holy trinity that would hold up the new economic order, the other two being the International Monetary Fund (IMF), which promoted ever freer global capital flows, and the World Bank, which would supervise the transformation of developing countries along free market lines and manage their integration into the global economy.

Multilateralism in Disarray

Yet even as the prophets of globalization talked about the in-creasing obsolescence of the nation-state, the main beneficiary of the new post-Cold War global order was the United States.

Though it was supposedly a mechanism for freer trade, the WTO's most important agreements promoted monopoly for US firms: the Trade-Related Intellectual Property Rights Agreement (TRIPs) consolidated the hold over high-tech innovations by US corporations such as Intel, Microsoft and Monsanto, while the Agreement on Agriculture institutionalized a system of monopolistic competition for third-country markets between the agribusiness interests of the United States and the European Union.

When the Asian financial crisis engulfed countries that had been seen by many in the business community as America's most formidable competitors, Washington did not try to save the Asian economies by promoting expansionary policies. Instead, it used the IMF to dismantle the structures of state-assisted Asian capitalism that had been regarded as formidable barriers to the entry of goods and investments from US transnationals that had been clamouring vociferously to get their piece of the 'Asian miracle'. It was less their belief in spreading the alleged benefits of free trade than maximizing geo-economic and geo-strategic advantage that lay behind US support for the policies of the IMF, World Bank and WTO.

Acting to achieve its interests under multilateral cover was the preferred US strategy for most of the post-war period, whether it was the Bretton Woods institutions, the United Nations or the Group of Seven that provided the framework for 'hegemonic leadership'. Yet when these institutions got in the way of US interests, Washington did not hesitate to act unilaterally. This was increasingly the case in the 1990s, with removal of the incentives for multilateral behaviour posed by Soviet competition.

The instrumental use of multilateral agencies was stark when it came to the UN. While using the United Nations to provide cover for its policy of isolating Iraq, Washington also refused to pay its dues to the UN owing to the influence of the Republican right, angry at the world body's not kowtowing wholeheartedly to US policy. Or the USA simply disregarded the UN when it could not get a mandate and proceeded to work its will through more pliable institutions, as it did when it resorted to NATO cover for the bombing of Yugoslavia during the Kosovo conflict in 1999.

The G-7 – later G-8 with the addition of Russia – emerged in the 1970s to provide a mechanism for more multilaterally shared decision-making among the advanced capitalist countries, especially in economic matters. Yet, especially under the administration of George W. Bush, Washington has embarked on a unilateralist course that has brought it into sharp conflict with other members on the burning issues of banning land mines, climate change, missile defence and reconciliation between the two Koreas. Washington's brusque junking of a painstakingly negotiated agreement, the Kyoto Protocol on Climate Change, marked a new low in unilateralist behaviour.

The G-8 was at its nadir when it held its annual summit in Genoa in July 2001, with over 200,000 people coming from Europe and all over the world to protest at the framework of neoliberalism with a good dose of American unilateralism that it was imposing on the globe.

The events of September 11, 2001 led some to expect a re-surgence of multilateralism as the USA sought to forge a global military alliance against terrorism. Co-operation between the USA and the European Union saved the Fourth Ministerial of the WTO in November 2001 from going the way of the Third Ministerial in Seattle, which had collapsed in disarray. Yet the Bush administration was back in fine unilateralist form a few months' later, as it withdrew from the newly formed International Criminal Court and signalled its determination not to renew the Anti-Ballistic-Missile Defense Treaty that Washington had negoti-ated with the Soviet Union in 1972.

The Crisis of the Neoliberal Order

Increasing resort to unilateralism and the brazen manipulation of multilateral mechanisms to achieve hegemony by the United States was an important source of the crisis of legitimacy that began to

grip the global order in the late 1990s. But equally important as
the erosion of multilateralism as a source of de-legitimation was
the spreading realization that the global neoliberal regime resting
on free trade and free markets could no longer deliver on its
promise. That the system could not create prosperity for all but
only the illusion of it was something that many observers had
known for some time. However, the realities of growing global
poverty and inequality were neutralized by the high growth rates
and the prosperity of a few enclaves of the world economy, like
East Asia in the 1980s, which were (mistakenly) painted as paragons
of market-led development. When the Asian economies collapsed
in the long hot summer of 1997, however, the follies of neoliberal
economics came to the fore. All the talk about the Asian financial
crisis being caused by crony capitalism could not obscure the fact
that it was the liberation of speculative capital from the constraints
of regulation, largely in response to pressure from the IMF, that
brought about East Asia's collapse. The IMF also came under
severe public scrutiny for imposing draconian programmes on the
Asian economies in the wake of the crisis – programmes that
merely accelerated economic contraction – while putting together
multi-billion-dollar rescue packages to save not the crisis economies, but foreign banks and speculative investors.

The IMF's role in East Asia triggered a re-examination of its
role in imposing structural adjustment programmes in much of
Africa, South Asia and Latin America in the 1980s, and the fact
that these programmes had, as they did in Asia, exacerbated
stagnation, widened inequalities and deepened poverty now became widely realized.

The Asian financial crisis triggered the unravelling of the
legitimacy of the IMF. In the case of the WTO, the situation was
even more dramatic. In the years following the founding of the
WTO in 1995, growing numbers of governments, communities
and social movements began to realize that in signing on to the
WTO, their governments had signed on to a charter for corporate
rule that consumer advocate Ralph Nader called the principle of

'trade über alles' – or trade above equity, justice, environment
and practically everything else they held dear. Many developing
country governments discovered that in signing on, they had
signed away their rights to development. The many streams of
discontent and opposition converged in the streets of Seattle at
the end of November 1999 to bring down the Third Ministerial
meeting of the WTO and trigger a severe institutional crisis that
continues to this day.

Also dragged into the line of fire was the World Bank, which
an investigating group reporting to the US House of Representatives, the Meltzer Commission, accused, in early 2000, of
being irrelevant to the task of eliminating poverty.

Not surprisingly, in the face of criticism coming from the right
to the left, reform of the multilateral system became prominent in
the rhetoric of the multilateral agencies and the G-7 governments
that were their most powerful backers. Debt forgiveness, a new
global financial architecture, reform of the decision-making structures of the WTO and the Bretton Woods institutions were among
the high-profile promises that generated expectations that change
was finally on the way. Five years after the crisis, however, there
has been zero change in the policies and structures of these
institutions.

The Corporation under Question

By the end of the last decade of the twentieth century, in short,
the triumphalism that marked the beginning of the decade had
evaporated and given way to a deep crisis of legitimacy of the
multilateral order. Accompanying that crisis were swiftly rising
levels of resentment against the prime engine of globalization:
the corporation.

Several factors came together to focus public attention on the
corporation in the 1990s – the most egregious being the preda-
tory practices of Microsoft, the environmental depredations of
Shell, the irresponsibility of Monsanto and Novartis in promoting

genetically modified organisms, Nike's systematic exploitation of dirt-cheap labour, and Mitsubishi, Ford and Firestone's conceal-ment from consumers of serious product defects.

A sense of environmental emergency was also spreading by the beginning of the twenty-first century, and to increasing numbers of people, the rapid melting of the polar ice caps could be traced to Big Oil and the automobile giants' continuing promotion of an environmentally destabilizing petroleum civilization, and, more generally, to the process of uncontrolled growth driven by the transnational corporations (TNCs).

Ironically, in the United States, it was during the apogee of the so-called New Economy that the distrust of the corporation was at its highest in decades. According to a *Business Week* survey, '72 per cent of Americans say business has too much power over their lives.' [1] And the magazine warned: 'Corporate America, ignore these trends at your peril.'[2]

Members of the global elite with antennae sensitive to the rumblings underneath took such warnings seriously, and the annual meeting of the World Economic Forum (WEF) in Davos, Switzerland, became the venue to elaborate a response that would go beyond the bankrupt strategy of denying that corporate-driven globalization was creating tremendous problems to promote a strategy that would 'bring the fruits of globalization and free trade to the many', as British Prime Minister Tony Blair put it.[3] Yet the task was formidable, for it became increasingly clear that in an unregulated global market, it was even more difficult to reconcile the demands of social responsibility with the demands of profit-ability. The best that 'globalization with a conscience' could offer was, as C. Fred Bergsten, a noted pro-globalization advocate admitted, a system of 'transitional safety nets ... to help the adjustment to dislocation' and enable people to 'take advantage of the phenomenon [of globalization] and roll with it rather than oppose it'.[4]

Cracks in Military Hegemony

Corporate power is one dimension of global power. But there is, equally of consequence, strategic power, and this, even more than corporate power, is concentrated in the United States. Strategic power cannot be reduced, as in orthodox Marxism, to simply being determined by the dynamics of corporate control. The US state cannot be reduced simply to being a servant of US capital. The Pentagon has its own dynamics, and one cannot understand the US role in the Balkans or its changing posture towards China as simply determined by the interests of US corporations. Indeed, in Asia, it has been strategic extension, not corporate expansion, that has been the mainspring of US policy, at least until the mid-1980s. And, in the case of China, US capital's desire to exploit the fabled 'China market' has increasingly found itself in opposition to the Pentagon's definition of China as the Enemy, which must be headed off at the pass instead of being assisted by western investment to become a full-blown threat. In many instances, indeed, corporate power and state power may not be in synch.

Having said this, it is none the less a primordial aim of the transnational US garrison state that is ensconced deeply in East Asia, the Middle East and Europe and projects power to the rest of the globe, to manage a global order that secures the primacy of US corporations. *New York Times* columnist Thomas Friedman may be wrong about the benign impact of globalization, but he is definitely on target when he asserts that: 'The hidden hand of the market will never work without a hidden fist. McDonald's cannot flourish without McDonnell Douglas, the designer of the US Air Force F-15. And the hidden fist that keeps the world safe for Silicon Valley's technologies to flourish is called the US Army, Air Force, Navy, and Marine Corps.'[5]

With the growing illegitimacy of corporate-driven globalization and the growing divide between a prosperous minority and an increasingly marginalized majority, military intervention to maintain the global status quo is becoming a constant feature of international relations, whether this is justified in terms of fighting drugs, fighting terrorism, containing 'rogue states', 'containing China', or of opposing 'Islamic fundamentalism'. These interventions are deeply unpopular in the Third World, so that when the Al Qaeda hijackers flew their planes into the World Trade Center and the Pentagon on September 11, many people in the South were caught between revulsion at the resulting mayhem and a feeling that the USA 'had it coming'. Moreover, a US security system that had seemed invulnerable now looked very vulnerable indeed to a resentful world.

To many people in Europe and Japan, the role of US military as the guarantor of their security still prevails. But it is a sentiment that is fast eroding. The collapse of Soviet power created the condition for reassessment by Washington's allies of the role of US power. Doubts have increased with the Pentagon's insistence on building a missile defence system against potential rather than real enemies while preparing the ground for a new Cold War crusade against China. And recently, even as many traditional allies enlisted in the so-called 'war against terror', US unilateralism is undermining old alliances as Washington prepares the ground to invade Iraq, even against the express wishes of most members of the European Union. Loss of trust in Washington is the source of moves to create a European defence force that would operate with some independence of NATO.

A far-flung system of bases and the ability to project force into every corner of the world such as that possessed by Washington are usually seen as indicators of tremendous strength. This 'strength', however, can turn into a weakness: that of over-extension or a growing gap between resources and capabilities. And, as will be shown below, over-extension of US strategic power became a very real condition after September 11.

The Degeneration of Liberal Democracy

It is not, however, corporate power or military power that has traditionally been the USA's strongest asset but, following the thinking of Antonio Gramsci, its ideological power – its 'soft power'.

The USA is a Lockean democracy – that is, its foundation is the political philosophy of the late-seventeenth-century English thinker John Locke – and its ability to project its mission as the extension of systems centred on free elections to choose governments devoted to promoting liberal rights and freedoms continues to be a strong source of its legitimacy in many parts of the world. The trend away from authoritarian regimes and towards formal democracy in the Third World happened in spite of rather than because of the United States. Yet, especially under the Clinton administration, Washington was able to jibe skilfully to catch the democratic winds, in the process reconstructing its image from being a supporter of repressive regimes to being an opponent of dictatorships.

In the last few years, however, Washington- or Westminster-style democracies – or, as William Robinson calls them, 'polyarchies'[6] – with their focus on formal rights and formal elections and their bias against economic equality achieved through such measures as asset and income redistribution, have degenerated into increasingly stagnant and polarized political systems, such as those in the Philippines, Brazil and Pakistan, so that some theorists have raised the question as to whether or not the so-called 'third wave of democratization' is over.

What was of great significance, however, was the fact that democracy was also entering into crisis in the oldest modern democracy. Interest-group influence, which the Washington style of electoral competition had institutionalized, reached massive proportions. In the 1980s and 1990s, increasing numbers of Americans began to realize that their liberal democracy had been so thoroughly corrupted by corporate money politics that it deserved to be designated a 'plutocracy'. Indeed, as William Pfaff noted, 'nothing on the scale of the American system of political expenditure and influence exists anywhere'.[7] Campaign finance reform was the hot issue that propelled the candidacy of Senator

John McCain, who made a strong run for the Republican nomination in the spring of 2000.

Corporate money combined with constitutional rules designed to restrict majority rule to create a situation in which the man who lost the popular vote – and, according to some, the electoral college vote as well – ended up as president of the world's most powerful liberal democracy. This has triggered deep disaffection with what is now universally regarded as an outmoded, ancient, complex system of protecting private interests from public power and restraining the 'passions' of the majority.

The deeply corrupting role of corporate money in political life is not the only burning issue. There are also the urban crisis, a class gulf exacerbated by free trade and capital mobility, severe inequities of distribution of income among the industrial countries, a racial crisis posing as a law-and-order problem, the 'cultural civil war' between fundamentalists and liberals, and the increasing power of the military.

This last phenomenon is worth singling out, since it illustrates the increasing inability of the system to deal with the new realities of power. While, in classic Montesquieuesque fashion, Congress and the Executive were busy checkmating each other on the issue of former President Clinton's sexual mores, both institutions were unable to cope with the accumulation of political power on the part of the Pentagon. As a consequence, as one insightful commentator pointed out, the 'military is already the most powerful institution in American government, in practice largely unaccountable to the executive branch. Now the armed forces are setting the limits of American foreign policy…The United States is not yet 18th-century Prussia, when the military owned the state, but the threat is more serious than most Americans realize.'[8]

To a world that had long been told about the superiority of the American way, the last decade has revealed the flaws of a system designed to enhance private, corporate power and limit the countervailing power of the state, to put infinite obstacles in the way of public power and the popular will achieving socially progressive ends. The following comments of Daniel Lazare in his influential book *The Frozen Republic* are widely shared:

> Government in America doesn't work because it's not supposed to work. In their infinite wisdom, the Founders created a deliberately unresponsive system in order to narrow the governmental options and force us to seek alternative routes. Politics were dangerous; therefore, politics had to be limited and constrained. But America cannot be expect to survive much longer with a government that is inefficient and none too democratic in design. It is impossible to forge ahead in the late twentieth century using governmental machinery dating from the late eighteenth. Urban conditions can only worsen, race relations can only grow more poisonous, while the middle class can only grow alienated and embittered.[9]

The crisis of liberal democracy is not limited to the South and the United States. There is also a deepening crisis of democratic governance in Europe, brought on partly by the increasing captivity of party politics to money politics, as the bribery scandal involving Helmut Kohl and the Christian Democratic Party in Germany and the ascent of Italy's most powerful capitalist, Silvio Berlusconi, to the apex of government illustrate.

But there is as well another, related cause of disaffection, and this is the non-transparent process that technocratic elites allied to corporate elites have, in the name of European integration, technocratic rationality and market rationality, eroded the principle of subsidiarity by funnelling effective political and economic decision-making power upwards to techno-corporate structures at the apex of which stands the European Commission, that are largely unaccountable to electorates on the ground.

As George Ross pointed out, from the origins, the process of building the European economic and political system 'was consciously elitist'.[10]

> For everyone to benefit, European construction had to proceed in the shadows of democratic accountability as ordinarily understood. After 1985 the Commission and others had little choice but to

work within a European institutional system reflecting this philosophy. There was an appointed Commission empowered with
sweeping powers of policy proposition. There were secretive and
opaque councils of ministers, an imperious European Council, and
a powerful European Court of Justice. Then there was an impotent
talking shop of a parliament. Connections among these institutions
and any mass European political culture were tenuous. Moreover,
they were all knit into a system whose operations were per-
plexingly complicated and largely unfathomable to nonspecialists.[11]

In retrospect, the revolt of the Danish electorate against the
Maastricht Treaty in 1992 was simply the first salvo of a populist
revolt whose most recent dramatic manifestation was the massive
voter disaffection against technocratic politics wielded in the
name of 'European Unity' that allowed the neo-fascist Jean-Marie
Le Pen to oust Prime Minister Lionel Jospin during the first
round of the French presidential elections in April 2002.

The Spectre of Global Deflation

What makes the crisis of legitimacy of the key institutions of the
global economic and political system so volatile from the point
of view of the elites of the North is that it is intersecting with a
profound structural crisis of the global economy.

The G-7 came into existence to co-ordinate the macroeconomic policies of the rich countries in order to navigate between
the Scylla of inflation and the Charybdis of stagnation. In the last
few years, however, efforts to synchronize fiscal and monetary
initiatives have proved ineffective, and what modicum of co-
operation was achieved has failed to bring Japan out of a decade-
long recession or to prevent the onset of a new global recession.

The basic reason for this failure has been the reluctance of
public authorities to regulate the activity of capital in the new
global economy. With corporate-driven market forces unchecked,
structural imbalances built up. The boom of the early and mid-
1990s resulted in a burst of global investment activity that led to

tremendous over-capacity all around.[12] The indicators are stark. The US computer industry's capacity has been rising at 40 per cent annually, far above projected increases in demand. The world auto industry is now selling just 74 per cent of the 70.1 million cars it builds each year. So much investment took place in global telecommunications infrastructure that traffic carried over fibre-optic networks is reported to be only 2.5 per cent of capacity. There is, says economist Gary Shilling, an 'oversupply of nearly everything'.[13]

Profits apparently stopped growing in the US corporate sector after 1997, leading firms to a wave of mergers, the main purpose of which was the elimination of competition. The most prominent of these were the Daimler Benz–Chrysler–Mitsubishi union, the Renault takeover of Nissan, the Mobil–Exxon merger, the BP–Amoco–Arco deal, and the blockbuster 'Star Alliance' in the airline industry.

In addition to mergers, another avenue that was taken to avoid the crisis of profitability in industry was to push investment to speculative activity, notably to the stockmarket and the real-estate sector, leading to the spectacular boom and bust in East Asia in the 1990s. At the time of the Asian crisis - which, incidentally, has not been surmounted – many observers pointed out that it was the same hothouse speculation that underpinned the Wall Street–Silicon Valley complex that drove the US economy. What optimists – the most prominent being US Federal Reserve Board Chairman Alan Greenspan – called the 'New Economy' seemed for a time to defy the laws of economics, with Internet stars such as Amazon.com registering an explosive and seemingly permanent rise in stock values even as they continued to operate at a loss.

But all talk about the emergence of a New Economy vanished when the law of gravity caught up with the speculative sector in the late 1990s, resulting in the wiping out of $4.6 trillion in investor wealth in Wall Street, a sum that, as *Business Week* pointed out, was half of the US Gross Domestic Product and four times the wealth wiped out in the 1987 crash.[14]

According to Gary Shilling and a number of other pessimists, probably the reason the macroeconomic imbalances are working themselves out in what is likely to be a deeper than expected recession is that we are now at the downward curve of the so-called 'Kondratieff Cycle'. Proposed by the Russian economist Nikolai Kondratieff, this theory suggests that the progress of global capitalism is marked not only by short-term business cycles but by long-term 'supercycles'. Kondratieff cycles are roughly fifty- to sixty-year-long waves. The upward curve of the Kondratieff cycle is marked by the intensive exploitation of new technologies, followed by a crest as technological exploitation matures, then a downward curve as the old technologies produce diminishing returns while new technologies are still in an experimental stage in terms of profitable exploitation; finally there is a trough or prolonged deflationary period.

The trough of the last wave was in the 1930s and 1940s, a period marked by the Great Depression and World War II. The ascent of the current wave began in the 1950s and the crest was reached in the 1980s and 1990s. The profitable exploitation of the post-war advances in the key energy, automobile, petrochemical and manufacturing industries ended while that of information technology was still at a relatively early stage. From this perspective, the 'New Economy' of the late 1990s was not a transcendence of the business cycle, as many economists believed it to be, but the last glorious phase of the current supercycle before the descent into prolonged deflation. In other words, the uniqueness of the current conjuncture lies in the fact that the downward curve of the current short-term cycle coincides with the move into descent of the Kondratieff supercycle.

Marxists say that what underlies such conjunctures is that the old 'relations of production' or the complex of existing capitalist property relations and institutions, come into conflict with the further development of the 'forces of production' or technologies, which is possible only if this process is no longer driven by the search for profit.

Is the world in for a bout with more than a normal recession? To use Joseph Schumpeter's terms, is the global economy moving into a prolonged period of 'creative destruction'?

By mid-2002, talk about a 'short' US recession disappeared as businesses continued to refrain from investing, the stock market continued on its downward path, and revelations of Wall Street crime dominated the news. Prolonged stagnation also appeared to be the fate of Europe and much of the rest of the world, with practically only China and South Korea bucking the trend. People began to realize that with the integration of economies in an era of rapid globalization there also came the spectre of synchronized depression.

The Rise of the Movement

In retrospect, with the deepening crisis of legitimacy of the prime institutions of the global system in the latter half of the 1990s, Seattle was a cataclysm waiting to happen, though most of the elites benefiting from globalization were clueless about the depth of the resentment and rage they had provoked. The hurricane of people's protest moved on to Washington during the World Bank-IMF spring meeting in April 2000; Chiang Mai in Thailand, during the Asian Development Bank annual meeting in May 2000; Melbourne during the World Economic Forum gathering in early September 2000; and Prague during the World Bank-IMF annual meeting in late September 2000.

While a beleaguered global elite assembled in Davos in late January 2001 to ponder the meaning of the burgeoning 'anti-globalization movement', some 12,000 representatives of inter-national civil society met in Porto Alegre, Brazil, to declare that 'another world is possible'. Davos, or the World Economic Forum, had found its political and ideological nemesis in the World Social Forum. Celebration of the power of the movement was one aspect of Porto Alegre; the other was planning and gathering strength for future action. Tens of thousands besieged the Summit of the Americas in Quebec City in late April 2001 and the European Union Summit in Gothenburg in late June. And despite outright police assaults using teargas, armed personnel carriers and provocateurs, over 200,000 people isolated the G-8 annual meeting in the ancient city of Genoa in late July 2001.

Nowhere was the crisis of legitimacy of the global system more evident than in Genoa, where the leaders of the top Northern economies had to admit that meeting in places accessible to people had become almost impossible. Not surprisingly, the desert kingdom of Qatar was designated the site of the Fourth Ministerial of the WTO in November 2001 while a remote ski resort high up in the Canadian Rockies was chosen to host the next G-8 meeting in July 2002.

Contradictory Trends after September 11

Then came September 11, and with it a massive effort on the part of the pro-globalization forces, who now saw the whole thing as a war, to turn the tide by trying to extend the range of terrorist action to include the civil disobedience tactics of anti-corporation globalization activists, and, even more important, by manipulating the anti-terrorist hysteria to ram through the liberalization agenda at the Fourth Ministerial of the WTO in Doha, Qatar. The establishment media got into the act and wrote off the movement as 'dead'.

But in politics and in war, fortune smiles all too briefly. After allowing it briefly to savour the apparent success of its invasion of Afghanistan in late 2001, history, cunning and inscrutable as usual, suddenly dealt the Bush administration two massive body blows: the Enron implosion and the Argentine collapse. These twin disasters threatened to push the global elite back to the crisis of legitimacy that was threatening its hegemony globally prior to September 11.

Capitalist crisis and corporate fraud Enron forcefully reminded the world that free market rhetoric is a corporate con game. Neo-liberalism loves to couch itself in the language of efficiency and the ethics of the greatest good for the greatest number, but it is really about promoting corporate power. Enron lavishly extolled the so-called merits of the market to explain its success, but in fact, its path to becoming the USA's seventh largest corporation was paved not by following the discipline imposed by the market but by strategically deploying cold cash, and lots of it. Enron literally bought its way to the top, throwing around hundreds of millions of dollars in less than a decade to create what one businessman described to the *New York Times* as the 'black hole' of deregulated energy markets in which its financial shenanigans could thrive unchecked.[15] To make sure government would look the other way and allow the 'market' to have its way, Enron was generous with those willing to serve it, and few earned more Enron dollars than George W. Bush, who received some $623,000 for his political campaigns in both Texas and nationally from his friend Kenneth Lay, Enron CEO.

The deep enmeshing of Bush and a number of his key lieuten-ants in Enron's corporate web has shaken off George W's post-September 11 image of being president of all Americans and brought back the reality of his being the chief executive officer of corporate America. The Enron scandal pulled Americans right back to the bitter *sozialepolitik* of the 1990s when, as Bush himself put it in his inaugural speech, 'it seems we share a continent but not a country'.[13] It brought back the ideological context of the landmark electoral campaign of 2000 when Bush's fellow Repub-lican, John McCain, made an almost successful bid to become the presidential standard-bearer by focusing on one issue: that the massive corporate financing of elections that had transformed US democracy into a plutocracy was gravely undermining its legitimacy.

Corporate-driven globalization is a process marked by massive corruption and deeply subversive of democracy. Shell in Nigeria was a good case study. Scores of TNCs and the World Bank were implicated with the Suharto political economy in Indonesia. Now Enron stripped the veil from what Wall Street used to call the 'New Economy', which showered rewards on sleazy financial operators like Enron while sticking the rest of the world with the costs.

As 2002 rolled on, Enron was, in fact, revealed to be merely the tip of the iceberg. In quick succession, Wall Street pillars such as the accounting giant Arthur Andersen and investment banker Merrill Lynch or Wall Street darlings such as Tyco International, Rite Aid, Global Crossing, Martha Stewart Living Omnimedia, Adelphia Communications and Worldcom were shown to have either rigged their accounts to show profits or engaged in other fraudulent practices.

But Enron and its ilk were products not simply of unfettered deregulation but of something more fundamental: the crisis of overcapacity in a system of finance-driven global capitalism. As noted earlier, the crisis of overcapacity led to a loss of profitability by the late nineties, triggering a wave of mergers seeking to restore profitability via the elimination of competition or from some mystical process called 'synergy'. In actual fact, many mergers ended up consolidating costs without adding to profitability, as was the case, for instance, with the much-ballyhooed America Online–Time Warner deal.

With profit margins slim or nonexistent, survival increasingly meant greater and greater dependence on Wall Street financing, which came increasingly under the sway of hybrid investment-commercial bankers such as JP Morgan Chase, Salomon Barney Smith and Merrill Lynch, which competed aggressively to put together deals. With little to show in terms of an attractive bottom line, some firms took the route of trading future promise for hard cash in the present, something that creative investment managers were especially good at in the high-tech sector. It was this seemingly innovative technique of trading on illusion that resulted in the stratospheric rise of share values in the high-tech sector, where they lost all relation to the real state of companies. Many 'start-ups' lost all connection to production and served mainly as mechanisms to inflate share prices to enable venture capitalists and managers with stock options to make a killing from an early sale, after which the firm was left to languish and eventually collapse.

However, trading on illusion could only get you so far. In the end, there was no getting around the fact that your balance sheet had to show an excess of revenue over costs to continue to attract investors. This was the simple but harsh reality that led to the proliferation of fancy accounting techniques such as that of Enron finance officer Andrew Fastow's 'partnerships', which were mechanisms to keep major costs and liabilities off the balance sheet, as well as cruder methods such as Worldcom's masking of current costs as capital expenditures.

In the context of deregulation and the benign approach to the private sector that accompanied the reigning neoliberal, 'hands-off-business' outlook, it was easy for such pressures to erode the so-called 'firewalls' – between management and board, stock analyst and stockbroker, auditor and audited. Faced with the common spectre of an economy on the downspin and slimmer pickings for all, the watchdogs and the watched threw off the pretence of being governed by a system of checks and balances, and united to promote the illusion of prosperity – and thus maintain the financial lifeline to unsuspecting investors – as long as possible.

This united front could not be maintained for long, however, since it was very tempting for those who knew the real score to sell before the mass of investors got wise to what was happening. In the end, business acumen was reduced to figuring out when to sell, taking the money and running – and avoiding prosecution. Enron CEO Jeffrey Skilling read the handwriting on the wall, resigned, and made off with $112 million from the sale of his stock options a few months before the fall. Not so lucky was Tyco's Dennis Kozlowski, who was not content with raking off $240 million and was still trying to milk his cash cow when his company went under.

In sum, while there are villains aplenty, the so-called ethical crisis of the corporation is largely a symptom of a more funda-mental structural crisis rooted in the dynamics of finance-driven deregulated global capitalism.

The Argentine collapse What the corporate fraud was to the legitimacy of global capitalism in the North, the Argentine débâcle was to the globalist project in the South. Owing $140 billion to international institutions and with its economy plunged into chaos, Argentina is today in a truly pitiable state.

Argentina had been the poster-boy of globalization Latin-style. It brought down its trade barriers faster than most other countries in Latin America. It liberalized its capital account more radically. And in the most touching gesture of neoliberal faith, the Argentine government voluntarily gave up any meaningful control over the domestic impact of a volatile global economy by adopting a currency board, that is, pegging the peso to the dollar. Dollar-ization, some technocrats promised, was right around the corner and, when that happened, the last buffers between the local economy and the global market would disappear and the nation would enter the nirvana of permanent prosperity.

All of these measures were taken either at the urging of or with the approval of the US Treasury Department and its surro-gate, the International Monetary Fund. In fact, in the wake of the Asian financial crisis, when capital account liberalization was increasingly seen by most observers as the villain of the piece, Larry Summers, then Secretary of the Treasury, extolled Argen-tina's selling off of its banking sector as a model for the developing world: 'Today, fully 50 per cent of the banking sector, 70 per cent of private banks, in Argentina are foreign-controlled, up from 30 per cent in 1994. The result is a deeper, more efficient market, and external investors with a greater stake in staying put.'[16]

As the dollar rose in value in the mid-1990s, so did the peso, making Argentine goods uncompetitive both globally and locally. Raising tariff barriers against imports flooding in was regarded as a no-no. Instead, borrowing heavily to fund the dangerously widening trade gap, Argentina spiralled into debt, and the more it borrowed, the higher the interest rates rose as creditors grew increasingly alarmed at the consequences of the unbridled market freedom from which they had initially benefited.

Contrary to the Summers doctrine, foreign control of the banking system was no panacea. In fact, foreign control simply facilitated the outflow of much-needed capital by banks that became increasingly reluctant to lend to both government and local businesses. With no credit, small and medium enterprises – and not a few big ones – closed down, throwing thousands out of work.

The crisis unfolded with frightening speed in December 2001. Cap in hand, Argentina went to its mentor, the IMF, for a multi-billion-dollar loan to meet payments on the $140 billion external debt coming due. In the grip of the old orthodoxy, the Fund refused unless the government made massive cuts in public expenditure and imposed a tight money policy. The standoff continues, even while the country spirals into chaos.

'Imperial Overstretch'

Meanwhile, on the military front, things were not looking so good for the world's sole remaining superpower by the middle of 2002.

Over eight months after the launching of the global war against terror, it became increasingly clear that the USA was caught in a relentlessly expanding conflict from which there is no easy withdrawal. Trying to keep up the momentum of its war against terror after it declared 'victory' in Afghanistan in early January, the USA sent troops to the Philippines that same month to help hunt down members of the Abu Sayyaf bandit group that it alleged had ties with Osama bin Laden's Al Qaeda network.

The Philippines, an ex-colony, seemed to be a convenient choice as a site for expanding the war against terror as Washington debated from January to March 2002 a far more important question: whether or not to take out Saddam Hussein. But just as the faction favouring an invasion of Iraq appeared to have gained the upper hand, the brutal Israeli sweep into the West Bank threw a spanner into US works, which had rested on the assumption of political support from the pro-USA Arab states.

Meanwhile, months after Washington's designating the Philippines a 'second front', some sixty to eighty Abu Sayyaf bandits continued to elude 6,000 Filipino troops coached by 160 US advisers on the small island of Basilan.

Moreover, the realities of the Afghanistan campaign that filtered out after the ousting of the Taliban punctured the triumphalist mood that had reigned a few months earlier. The idea that Afghanistan vindicated a new strategy of warfighting based on the employment of massive precision-guided airpower with little commitment of ground troops is now less persuasive. Thousands of civilians apparently died owing to less than precise bombing, and scores of people allied to the United States were targeted and killed by US forces acting on bad intelligence. Relying on Afghan mercenaries to do the fighting on the ground for the USA is now acknowledged by some in the Pentagon to have resulted in Osama bin Laden's escape from Afghanistan's Tora Bora mountains. And when US troops did engage in close-quarters fighting with the Taliban/Al Qaeda forces during 'Operation Anaconda', which took place in the Shah-i-kot area near Pakistan in early March, they were bloodied by an enemy that was supposed to be on the run.[17]

Though by mid-2002 it has not achieved its prime objective of capturing bin Laden or dismantling the Al Qaeda network – which was, in classic guerrilla fashion, retreating to its rear base along the border area of Pakistan – Washington still thinks it has the strategic initiative. It seemed to be the case, however, that it had launched itself into a multi-front war of attrition where it could not consolidate victory on any front.

The momentum was also being lost on the political front. As the military campaign lessened in intensity in Afghanistan, the United Nations was brought in to broker a political settlement that would usher in representative democracy while the European Union was dragged in to police the peace via a British-led armed contingent. It became clear, however, that the centralized authority that had been forged by the Taliban has given way to the return of warlord hegemony in different parts of the country, and the role of the security force is increasingly to keep the ex-partners in the Northern Alliance from cutting each other's throats. When the much vaunted *Loya Jirga* elections to produce a representative assembly ended up as a battle for spoils among warlords in early June 2002, 'quagmire' become a word that was more and more frequently used in the US press to describe the Afghan situation.

As Afghanistan slid into anarchy, Pakistan's strongman General Pervez Musharraf was destabilized and delegitimized by American pressure to take sides in the war against terror. The prestige of Islamic fundamentalists among the population was probably greater by mid-2002 than before September 11, 2001. Saudi Arabia was seething with discontent, and Washington faced the unpleasant prospect of having to serve ultimately as a police force between an increasingly isolated Saudi elite and a restive youthful population that regards bin Laden as a hero.

Washington's tilt towards Israel has not helped in shoring up the legitimacy of its Arab allies, including Egypt's Hosni Mubarak, among their peoples. Israel is the great spoiler of the US effort to manage the Middle East, and it can get away with it because it can rely on its massive support in the US Congress to blunt pressure from the US executive, as the brazen Israeli moves to destroy the Palestinian Authority in defiance of calls from Washington to end its military incursions into the West Bank demonstrated. With Washington's embrace of Israel's policy of forcing out Yasser Arafat as the head of the Palestinian people in late June 2002, the alliance that conservative Arab governments maintained with Washington became extremely difficult to justify to the Arab masses.

Indeed, the Afghan fiasco and Israeli intransigence, it can be argued, have combined to make Washington's strategic situation in the Middle East worse rather than better. Nor have there been any political or military gains in Southeast Asia, with Indonesia maintaining its distance from Washington and the US build-up in the Philippines turning out to be an open-ended commitment, like Vietnam. Indeed, post-September 11, political Islam appeared to have made significant gains among the Muslim populations of Indonesia, Malaysia, Thailand and the Philippines.

The introduction of US forces in Georgia and some of the Central Asian republics – the so-called 'Stans' – may, on the surface, seem to be a strategic plus, especially when one takes into consideration the energy reserves of the area. With the failure to achieve decisive military or political victory on any front, however, Washington's Central Asian deployments were actually stretching US power, with little real strategic gain.

Not surprisingly, there have emerged, in Washington, voices that now question whether the USA has the troops and resources to engage in a multi-front war of attrition. An invasion of Iraq, even if it did oust Saddam Hussein, would merely exacerbate the dilemma of over-extension, since military engagement in Iraq, as in Afghanistan, offered no easy exit from the massive political mess it would create. Paul Kennedy had a colourful phrase for Washington's emerging dilemma: 'imperial overstretch'.[18]

One was tempted to say, in fact, that there was a historical parallel to the USA's indiscriminate creation of new fronts against terror, and that was the Japanese rampage through Southeast Asia and the Pacific in the first six months of 1942. Large swathes of territory were gained, but at the price of over-extending Japanese imperial power. By creating so many fronts, Japan ended up unable to concentrate its forces and attention on the few really strategic sectors.

Liberal Democracy Loses

By mid-2002, there were no clear winners so far in the so-called war against terror. But there were clear losers. The Taliban was one. The other big loser was liberal democracy in the United

States, whose representativeness, as noted earlier, was already widely doubted prior to September 11. Not even the Cold War was presented in such totalistic terms as the 'War against Terror'. Laws and executive orders restricting the rights to privacy and free movement have been passed with a speed and in a manner that would have turned Joe McCarthy green with envy. The United States was scarcely three months into the war when legislation had already been passed and executive orders signed that established secret military tribunals to try non-US citizens; imposed guilt by association on immigrants; launched a massive effort to track down 8,000 young Muslim men; authorized the attorney-general to lock up aliens indefinitely on mere suspicion; expanded the use of wiretaps and secret searches; allowed the use of secret evidence in immigration proceedings that aliens cannot confront or rebut; gave the Justice Department the authority to overrule immigration judges; destroyed the secrecy of the client–lawyer relationship by allowing the government to listen in; and institutionalized racial and ethnic profiling.

Americans have often prided themselves on having a political system whose role is to maximize and protect individual liberty along the lines propounded by John Locke and Thomas Jefferson. That Lockean-Jeffersonian tradition was severely eroded in the months following September 11, as the ruling Republicans launched a drive to stampede the American people into granting government vast new powers over the individual in the name of guaranteeing order and security. Instead of moving to the future, America's limited democracy was regressing in its inspiration from the late-seventeenth-century Locke to the early-sixteenth-century Hobbes, whose masterwork *Leviathan* held that citizens owe unconditional loyalty to a state that guarantees the security of their life and limb.

The extent to which efforts to curtail traditional formal liberties were threatened was illustrated during a memorable Senate hearing when Attorney-General John Ashcroft said that critics of the Bush administration's security measures were fearmongers 'who scare peace-loving people with phantoms of lost liberty [and] aid terrorists'.[19] The fact that liberal, Democrat senators against whom these remarks were directed dared not respond shows how skilfully the conservatives had used the anti-terrorist struggle to win what they regarded to be the real war at home, which is the war against liberals and progressives. It is only recently that the opposition Democrats have moved to speak against curtailment of civil liberties, and rather timidly at that.

Already in crisis before September 11, American liberal democracy has been plunged into a deeper crisis of credibility by the post-September 11 moves of the ruling Republican right. Though many liberals and progressives are still strait-jacketed by the popularity of the anti-terrorist campaign, it is likely that as it becomes evident that the main intent of this campaign is to manage domestic dissent and drive a domestic counter-revolution, the 'cultural civil war' between liberals and conservatives will become less and less civil.

Porto Alegre and the Future

In sum, in a little over a decade, global capitalism has passed from triumph to crisis. September 11, in retrospect, was a slight reversal of this prolonged crisis, but the widening cracks in the system of global capitalism – including the liberal democratic political regimes and American military hegemony that act as its protective canopy – cannot be papered over for long. At this point, the crisis is principally a crisis of legitimacy. Crises of legitimacy, however, are a necessary prelude to change, since when legitimacy or consensus goes, it may only be a matter of time before the structures themselves unravel.

Yet the crisis of the system of global capitalism does not necessarily result in its replacement by a more benign alternative. Here it is important to retain a historical perspective. During the first phase of globalization, an era that spanned the nineteenth century and ended in 1914, the reaction to capitalism's inexorable commodification of the natural and social world was a search for community, for a new basis of social solidarity beyond the market. In retrospect, socialism, communism, social democracy and national liberation movements can all be seen as expressions of this countervailing thrust. Fascism, which Karl Polanyi defined as 'the reform of the market economy achieved at the price of the extirpation of democratic institutions',[20] was also part of this countervailing drive, one that hijacked the search for community in the service of reaction, counterrevolution, and racism.

Fascism nearly triumphed in the 1930s and early 1940s. But with its defeat during World War II, it was the struggle between two responses to unbridled free-market capitalism, Keynesian capitalism and state socialism, that dominated the greater part of the second half of the twentieth century. The Keynesian economic paradigm was actually a compromise among contending classes that placed limits on the operation of the market. Its widespread adoption by elites in both the North and the South – where it took the form of the 'developmental state' – was explained by the need to create a stable social base to contain global social revolution.

Similarly, the second phase of globalization, which began with the dismantling of the Keynesian state in the 1980s and reached its apogee in the mid-1990s, has provoked diverse expressions of a search for community, not all of them progressive. One of them is radical Islamism, which saw US corporate and military hegemony as the apogee of the long-running Western effort to erode the integrity of Islamic societies, reaffirmed the unity of the Islamic religion, people and state, and declared a *jihad* against the United States. Like fascism in the 1930s, its popular impact is not un-impressive: whatever one's ethical judgment of radical Islamism, it cannot be denied that by the end of the twentieth century it had succeeded in rallying the loyalty of large numbers of young people throughout the Islamic world, so much so that conservative ruling elites such as those in Pakistan and Saudi Arabia had to borrow its language in order to survive.

On the progressive side of the spectrum, diverse responses globally are coming together under the canopy of the 'Porto Alegre process'. The site of the World Social Forum (WSF) in 2001 and again in 2002, Porto Alegre, a medium-sized city in Brazil, has become the byword for the spirit of the burgeoning movement against corporate-driven globalization. Galvanized by the slogan 'Another world is possible', some 50,000 people flocked to this coastal city from January 30 to February 4, 2002. This figure was nearly five times the number of those who attended in 2001.

Fisherfolk from India, farmers from East Africa, trade unionists from Thailand, indigenous people from Central America were among those who made their way to Porto Alegre. Brazilians, of course, predominated in terms of numbers, but quite a number of Argentines crossed the River Plate to share their feelings about the tragedy in their country. There was also a sizeable contingent from the North, with Italy alone contributing over 2,000 delegates.

In symbolic terms, while Seattle was the site of the first major victory of the struggle against corporate-driven globalization, Porto Alegre represents the transfer to the South of the centre of gravity of what is now a surging global movement.

Now an annual affair, one might say that Porto Alegre performs three functions for this movement.

First, it represents a space – both physical and temporal – for this diverse global movement to meet, to network and, quite simply, to feel and affirm itself.

Second, it is a retreat during which the movement gathers its energies and charts the directions of its continuing drive to confront and roll back the processes, institutions and structures of global capitalism. For one cannot let up on the enterprise deconstructing the reigning structures. Naomi Klein, author of *No Logo*, put it simply but powerfully when she said that the need of the moment was 'less civil society and more civil disobedience'.[21]

Third, Porto Alegre provides a site and a space for the movement to paint, elaborate and debate the vision, values and institutions of an alternative world order. The centrepiece of the

2002 gathering were twenty-six plenary sessions over four days structured around four themes: 'the production of wealth and social reproduction', 'access to wealth and sustainable development', 'civil society and the public arena', and 'political power and ethics in the new society'. Around this core unfolded scores of seminars, a people's tribunal on debt, a convention of progressive parliamentarians, and about 500 workshops.

Porto Alegre, of course, was one moment of a larger process of charting alternatives. It was a macrocosm of so many smaller but equally significant enterprises going on throughout the world by millions who have told the reformists, cynics and 'realists' to move aside because indeed another world is possible. And necessary. At the beginning of the twentieth century, Rosa Luxemburg made her famous comment about the possibility that the future might belong to 'barbarism'. Barbarism in the form of fascism nearly triumphed six decades ago. Today, corporate-driven globalization is creating much of the same instability, resentment and crisis that serves as the breeding ground of fascist, fanatical and authoritarian populist forces. Globalization has not only lost its promise but it is embittering many. The forces representing genuine solidarity and community have no choice but to step in quickly and convince the disenchanted that another, better world is indeed possible, for the alternative is, as in the 1930s, seeing the vacuum filled by terrorists, demagogues of the religious and secular right and the purveyors of irrationality and nihilism.

Notes

1. 'Too Much Corporate Power', *Business Week*, September 11, 2000, p. 53.

2. 'New Economy, New Social Contract', *Business Week*, September 11, 2000, p. 80.

3. Speech at World Economc Forum, Davos, Switzerland, February, 2000.

4. C. Fred Bergsten, 'The Backlash Against Globalization', speech delivered at the 2000 meeting of the Trilateral Commission, Tokyo, April 2000 (downloaded from Internet).

5. Thomas Friedman, *The Lexus and the Olive Tree* (New York: Farrar Straus Giroux, 1999), p. 50.

6. See William Robinson, *Promoting Polyarchy: Globalization, US Intervention, and Hegemony* (Cambridge: Cambridge University Press, 1996).

7. William Pfaff, 'Money Politics is Winning the American Election', *International Herald Tribune*, March 11–12, 2000, p. 8.

8. William Pfaff, 'The Pentagon, not Congress or the President, Calls the Shots', *International Herald Tribune,* August 6, 2001.

9. Daniel Lazare, *The Frozen Republic: How the Constitution is Paralyzing Democracy* (New York: Harcourt Brace and Co., 1996), p. 5.

10. George Ross, 'Fin de Siècle Globalization, Democratization, and the Moore Theses: A European Case Study', in Theda Skocpol (ed.), *Democracy, Revolution, and History* (Ithaca, NY: Cornell University Press, 1998), p. 250.

11. Ibid.

12. See, among other works, Robert Brenner, 'The Economics of Global Turbulence', *New Left Review* 229 (May–June 1998) and A. Gary Shilling, *Deflation* (Short Hills, NJ: Lakeview Publishing Co., 1998).

13. Shilling, p. 177.

14. 'When Wealth is Blown Away', Business Week, March 26, 2001, p. 33.

15. Kurt Eichenwold, 'Enron's Collapse: Audacious Climb to Success Ended in Dizzying Plunge', *New York Times*, January 13, 2002.

16. Larry Summers, quoted in Walden Bello, 'Power, Timidity, and Irresponsibility in Global Finance', *Focus on Trade*, August 1999.

17. See 'The Valley of Death', *Time*, March 18, 2002.

18. See Paul Kennedy, *The Rise and Fall of the Great Powers* (New York: Vintage Books, 1989).

19. Quoted in Edward Klein, 'We're not Destroying Rights, We're Protecting Rights', *Parade Magazine,* May 19, 2002, p. 5.

20. Karl Polanyi, *The Great Transformation* (Boston: Beacon, 1957), p. 254.

21. Speech at the plenary 'Civil Society and the Public Arena', World Social Forum, Porto Alegre, Brazil, January 30–February 4, 2002.

TWO
Marginalizing the South in the International System

The issue of global economic governance has become extremely urgent in recent years. Alarm was registered during the Asian financial crisis in 1997, when the lack of regulations over global financial flows prevented the massive outflow of speculative capital from East and Southeast Asia, causing the collapse of these boom economies and great suffering to their peoples. The role of the International Monetary Fund (IMF) in making these economies vulnerable to volatile capital flows was severely criticized, as was its part in worsening the crisis of these economies with contractionary stabilization programmes in the aftermath of the speculative haemorrhage.

Following on the heels of the crisis of the IMF was the collapse of the Seattle ministerial of the World Trade Organization (WTO) in December 1999, which was caused by massive global disaffection with its policies of indiscriminate trade liberalization and with its non-transparent system of decision-making. Then, in February 2000, the International Financial Institution Advisory Commission appointed by the US Congress, better known as the Meltzer Commission, issued its report accusing the World Bank of being irrelevant to the problem of solving global poverty and the IMF of being part of the problem rather than the solution to global financial governance.

Who could have foreseen this severe crisis of legitimacy in the middle of the decade, when what was acknowledged as the pinnacle of the global multilateral system, the WTO, was born out of the eight-year Uruguay Round of trade negotiations? The future was bright and the challenge was 'coherence' in the multi-lateral system, that is, the synchronization of the policies of the World Bank, IMF and WTO to achieve the swiftest possible transition to a truly global economy based on free trade and financial flows. The grand vision was laid out in the WTO's famous 'Coherence Declaration':

> The interlinkages between the different aspects of economic policy require that the international institutions with responsibilities in each of these areas follow consistent and mutually supportive policies. The World Trade Organization should therefore pursue and develop cooperation with the international organizations responsible for monetary and financial matters, while respecting the mandate, the confidentiality requirements, and the necessary autonomy in decision-making procedures of each institution ... Ministers further invite the Director General of the WTO to review with the Managing Director of the International Monetary Fund and the President of the World Bank, the implications of the WTO's responsibilities for its cooperation with the Bretton Woods institutions, as well as the forms such cooperation might take, with a view to achieving greater coherence in global economic policymaking.[1]

By the year 2000, coherence was on the backburner, and the issue before the three institutions was their unravelling legitimacy and their ultimate survival.

The current system of global economic governance stems from the intersection of the two key dynamics of the post-World War II international economy: the competitive relations among the dominant capitalist economies and the efforts of the countries of the Third World to develop and push for a redistribution of global economic power. This analysis will focus on the latter.

The place to begin this analysis is the period of de-colonization in the 1950s and 1960s. The emergence of scores of newly in-dependent states took place in the politically charged atmosphere of the Cold War. Although they were often split between East and West in their political alliances, Third World countries gravitated towards an economic agenda that had two underlying thrusts: rapid development and a global redistribution of wealth.

While the more radical expression of this agenda in the shape of the Leninist theory of imperialism drew much attention and, needless to say, condemnation in some quarters, it was the more moderate version that was most influential in drawing otherwise politically diverse Third World governments into a common front. This was the vision, analysis and programme of action forged by Raul Prebisch, an Argentine economist who, from his base at the United Economic Commission for Latin America (CEPAL), won a global following with his numerous writings.

Developed in the late 1950s and early 1960s, Prebisch's theory centred on the worsening terms of trade between industrialized and non-industrialized countries, an equation which posited that more of the South's raw materials and agricultural products were needed to purchase fewer of the North's manufactured products. Moreover, the trading relationship was likely to get worse since Northern producers were developing substitutes for raw materials from the South, and Northern consumers would spend a decreasing proportion of their income on agricultural products from the South.[2]

The Rise of UNCTAD

Known in development circles as 'structuralism', Prebisch's theory of 'bloodless but inexorable exploitation', as one writer described it,[3] served as the inspiration for Third World organizations, formations and programmes that sprang up in the 1960s and 1970s. These included the Non-Aligned Movement, Group of 77, Organization of Petroleum Exporting Countries (OPEC) and the New International Economic Order (NIEO). It was also central to the establishment of the UN Conference on Trade and Development (UNCTAD) in 1964, which became over the next decade the principal vehicle used by the Third World countries in their effort to restructure the world economy.

With Prebisch as its first secretary-general, UNCTAD advanced a global reform strategy with three main prongs. The first was commodity price stabilization through the negotiation of price floors below which commodity prices would not be allowed to fall. The second was a scheme of preferential tariffs, or allowing Third World exports of manufactures, in the name of development, to enter First World markets at lower tariff rates than those applied to exports from other industrialized countries. The third was an expansion and acceleration of foreign assistance, which, in UNCTAD's view, was not charity but 'compensation, a rebate to the Third World for the years of declining commodity purchasing power'.[4] UNCTAD also sought to gain legitimacy for the Southern countries' use of protectionist trade policy as a mechanism for industrialization and demanded accelerated transfer of technology to the South.

To a greater or lesser degree, the structuralist critique came to be reflected in the approaches of other key economic agencies of the United Nations secretariat, such as the Economic and Social Council (ECOSOC) and the United Nations Development Program (UNDP), and became the dominant viewpoint among the majority at the General Assembly.

The Bretton Woods Twins versus the UN Development System

The response of the leading countries of the North to the challenge of economic de-colonization posed by the emerging countries was conditioned by several developments. Most important of these was the Cold War. The priority of the political enterprise of containing the Soviet Union and communism pushed the North, particularly the US government, to a less hardline stance when it came to the question of whether the economic structures of its client countries conformed to free market

principles. While the USA upheld private enterprise and demanded access for its corporations, it was more tolerant when it
came to protectionism, investment controls and a strong role for
government in managing the economy. It also veered away from
a classic exploitative stance to promote at least the image of
supporting limited global redistribution of wealth, this being
accomplished mainly through foreign aid. As the emerging
countries gravitated towards the UN system, the leading governments increasingly relied on the International Monetary Fund
(IMF) and the International Bank for Reconstruction and
Development (IBRD) to push their agenda.

The Bretton Woods institutions, founded in 1944, began with
missions quite distinct from their latter-day involvement with
North–South relations. The IMF was conceived by John Maynard
Keynes and Harry Dexter White, the two pillars of the Bretton
Woods meeting, as the guardian of global liquidity, a function
that it was supposed to fulfil by monitoring member countries'
maintenance of stable exchange rates and providing facilities on
which they could periodically draw to overcome cyclical balance
of payments difficulties. On the other hand, the IBRD was, as its
name implied, set up to assist in the reconstruction of the war-
torn economies, particularly those of Western Europe, by lending
to them at manageable rates of interest.

By the early 1970s, however, US President Richard Nixon's
taking the dollar off the gold standard had inaugurated a new era
of floating exchange rates that made the IMF's original mission
superfluous. Instead, the Fund was deeply involved in stabilizing
Third World economies with balance of payments difficulties. As
for the World Bank, it had evolved into the prime multilateral
development agency for aid and development.

In the case of the World Bank, a turning point of sorts was the
debate triggered by the 1951 report of a group of experts entitled
'Measures for the Economic Development of Under-Developed
Countries', which proposed making grant aid available to Third
World countries.[5] Using this as a springboard, Third World

countries at the General Assembly tried to push through resolutions that would establish the Special UN Fund for Economic Development (SUNFED), which would be controlled not by the North but by the UN and whose criterion for providing loans would not be narrow banking rules but development need.

The North, led by the United States, strenuously resisted these efforts, resorting at first to delay and diversion, such as proposing the creation of a $100 million fund to be used to finance an investment survey that the IBRD or some other Western agency would undertake.[6] But when diversion and delay failed to derail the South's drive to set up SUNFED, the North came out with an alternative: an institution for making soft loans for development from capital subscribed by the North but one controlled by the North rather than the Third World majority at the United Nations. Thus came into being the International Development Association (IDA), which was attached to the World Bank as the latter's soft-loan window. As one analyst of this period has pointed out:

> Much of the impetus for IDA came from the Bank itself, increasingly worried over Southern demands for a competing UN fund. Eugene R. Black, the bank's shrewd president, said bluntly that 'the International Development Association was really an idea to offset the urge for Sunfed'. Black, like any other banker, had little use for soft loans. But if anybody would make them, he reasoned, it had better be the Bank. If new business was to be done, Black wanted to do it.[7]

The IDA was part of a compromise package that effectively killed the idea of a UN-controlled development fund. The other part of the package was the establishment of the UN Special Fund, later renamed the UN Development Programme (UNDP), which served as the channel of much smaller quantities of mainly technical aid to Third World countries.[8]

The IDA–UNDP compromise derailed the demand for a UN-controlled agency, but it did not stop the escalation of Third World demands for a redistribution of global economic power.

This process resulted in the establishment of UNCTAD in 1964, and attained dramatic results with the Organization of Petroleum Exporting Countries' (OPEC) ability to seize control of oil pricing in the early and mid-1970s, culminating with the adoption by the UN General Assembly Special Session of 1974 of the 'new international economic order' programme. The thrust of these moves was clearly reformist rather than revolutionary, expressing demands of Third World elites rather than Third World masses. Nevertheless, their prominence in the context of successful struggles waged by revolutionary movements in Vietnam and other Third World countries lent a note of urgency to Washington's search for an effective counter-strategy of managed reform.

The Southern Challenge in the 1970s

In the 1970s, the World Bank was to be the centrepiece of liberal Washington's response. Robert McNamara, who was appointed in 1968 as the World Bank's president after his troubled stint at the US Defense Department, became the point man in the expanded liberal approach. The McNamara approach had several elements. First was a massive escalation in the World Bank's resources, with McNamara raising World Bank lending from an average of $2.7 billion a year when he took office in 1968, to $8.7 billion in 1978 and $12 billion by the time he left office in 1981. Second was a global programme aimed at ending poverty via a programme that sought to sidestep the difficult problems associated with social reform by focusing aid on improving the 'productivity of the poor'. Third was an effort to split the South by picking a few countries as 'countries of concentration' to which the flow of bank assistance would be higher than average for countries of similar size and income.

The rise of OPEC, however, made World Bank aid and foreign aid less critical to many of the leading countries in UNCTAD and the Group of 77 in the mid-1970s. These countries could gain access to massive quantities of loans that the commercial banks were only too happy to make available in their effort to turn a profit on the billions of dollars of deposits made to them by the OPEC countries.

Instead of aid, UNCTAD focused on changing the rules of international trade, and in this enterprise it registered some success. During the fourth conference of UNCTAD (UNCTAD IV) in Nairobi in 1976, agreement was reached, without dissent from the developed countries, on the Integrated Programme for Commodities (IPC). The IPC stipulated that agreements for eighteen specified commodities would be negotiated or renegotiated with the principal aim of avoiding excessive price fluctuations and stabilizing commodity prices at levels remunerative to the producers and equitable to consumers. It was also agreed that a common fund would be set up to regulate prices when they either fell below or climbed too far above the negotiated price targets.

UNCTAD and Group of 77 pressure was also central to the IMF's establishing a new window, the Compensatory Financing Facility (CFF), to assist Third World countries in managing foreign exchange crises created by sharp falls in the prices of the primary commodities they exported. Another UNCTAD achievement was getting the industrialized countries to accept the principle of preferential tariffs for developing countries. Some twenty-six developed countries were involved in sixteen separate 'general system of preference' schemes by the early 1980s.

These concessions were, of course, limited. In the case of commodity price stabilization, it soon became apparent that the rich countries had replaced a strategy of confrontation with an evasive strategy of frustrating concrete agreements. A decade after UNCTAD IV, only one new commodity stabilization agreement, for natural rubber, had been negotiated; an existing agreement on cocoa was not operative; and agreements on tin and sugar had collapsed.[9]

Right-Wing Reaction and the Demonization
of the South

By the late 1970s, however, even such small concessions were viewed with alarm by increasingly influential sectors of the US establishment. Such concessions within the UN system were seen in the context of other developments in North–South relations. These appeared to show that the strategy of liberal containment spearheaded by the Bank in the area of economic relations had not produced what it promised to deliver: security for Western interests in the South through the co-optation of Third World elites.

While professing anti-communism, governing elites throughout the Third World, which were the backbone of the UNCTAD system, gave in to popular pressure, abetted by local industrial interests, to tighten up on foreign investment. Nowhere did this trend spark more apprehension among American businesspeople than in two countries considered enormously strategic by US multinational firms. In Brazil, where foreign-owned firms accounted for half of total manufacturing sales,[10] the military-technocrat regime invoked national security considerations, and moved in the late 1970s to reserve the strategic information sector to local industries, provoking bitter denunciation from IBM and other US computer firms.[11] In Mexico, where foreign firms accounted for nearly 30 per cent of manufacturing output,[12] legal actions and threats of pulling investments by the powerful US drug industry followed the government's programme for the pharmaceutical industry. The industry proposed no-patent policies, promotion of generic medicines, local development of raw materials, price controls, discriminatory incentives for local firms and controls on foreign investment.[13]

Disturbing though these concessions and actions were, they could not compare in their impact with OPEC's second 'oil shock' in 1979. Despite the fact that Western oil companies were passing on the oil price increases to consumers in order to preserve their enormous profit margins, to many Americans OPEC became the symbol of the South: an irresponsible gang that was bent on using its near monopoly over a key resource in order to bring the West to its knees. Although OPEC was not dominated by communists or radical nationalists like Libya's Khadafy but by US allies such as Saudi Arabia, Kuwait and Venezuela, its 'oil weapon' evoked more apprehension than the nuclear arms of the Soviet Union. The oil cartel was feared as the precursor of a unified Southern bloc controlling most strategic commodities, and right-wing propagandists pointed to the Algiers Declaration of the Non-Aligned Movement in 1973 in their efforts to fan fear and loathing in the North: 'The heads of state or government recommend the establishment of effective solidarity organizations for the defense of the raw materials producing countries such as the Organization of Petroleum Exporting Countries ... to recover natural resources and ensure increasingly substantial export earnings.'[14]

The United Nations system was a central feature of the demonology of the South that right-wing circles articulated in the late 1970s and early 1980s. In their view, the UN had become the main vehicle for the South's strategy to bring about the New International Economic Order (NIEO). As the right-wing think-tank Heritage Foundation saw it, the governments of the South devoted 'enormous time and resources to spreading the NIEO ideology throughout the UN system and beyond. Virtually no UN agencies and bureaus have been spared.'[15] The South's effort to redistribute global economic power via UN mechanisms was viewed as a concerted one: private business data flows are under attack internationally and by individual Third World countries; proposals for strict controls of the international pharmaceutical trade are pending before more than one UN body; other international agencies are drafting restrictive codes of conduct for multinational corporations; and UNESCO has proposed international restraints on the press.[16]

Especially threatening to the Foundation was the effort by the Third World to 'redistribute natural resources' by bringing the seabed, space and Antarctica under their control through the Law of the Sea Treaty, the Agreement Governing Activities of States on the Moon and Other Celestial Bodies (called the Moon Treaty), and an ongoing UN study and debate over Antarctica. Malaysian Prime Minister Mahathir Bin Mohamad, the principal architect of the effort to get the UN to claim Antarctica, told the General Assembly 'all the unclaimed wealth of this earth' is the 'common heritage of mankind', and therefore subject to the political control of the Third World.[17]

Resubordinating the South

Structural adjustment When the Reagan administration came to power in 1981, it was riding on what it considered a mandate not only to roll back communism, but also to discipline the Third World. What unfolded over the next four years was a two-pronged strategy aimed at dismantling the system of 'state-assisted capitalism' that was seen as the domestic base for Southern national capitalist elites, and drastically weakening the United Nations system as a forum and instrument for the South's economic agenda.

The opportunity came none too soon in the form of the global debt crisis that erupted in the summer of 1982, which drastically weakened the capabilities of Southern governments in dealing with Northern states and corporations and Northern-dominated multilateral agencies. The instruments chosen for rolling back the South were the World Bank and the IMF. This was an interesting transformation for the World Bank, which had previously been vilified by the *Wall Street Journal* and the right wing as one of the villains behind the weakening of the North's global position by 'promoting socialism' in the Third World via its loans to Southern governments. But the liberal McNamara, who was now faulted by the right wing for losing in Vietnam and failing to contain the Southern challenge, was replaced by a more pliable successor, and ideological right-wingers seeking the closure of the Bank were restrained by pragmatic conservatives who wished to use the Bank instead as a disciplinary mechanism.

'Structural adjustment' referred to a new lending approach that had been formulated during McNamara's last years at the Bank. Unlike the traditional World Bank project loan, a structural adjustment loan was intended to push a programme of 'reform' that would cut across the whole economy or a whole sector of the economy. In the mid-1980s, IMF-1 and World Bank-imposed structural adjustment became the vehicle for a programme of free market liberalization that was applied across the board to Third World economies suffering major debt problems. Almost invariably, structural adjustment programmes had the following elements:

- Radically reducing government spending, ostensibly to control inflation and reduce the demand for capital inflows from abroad, a measure that in practice translated into cutting spending on health, education and welfare.
- Liberalizing imports and removing restrictions on foreign investment, ostensibly to make local industry more efficient by exposing them to foreign competition.
- Privatizing state enterprises and embarking on radical deregulation in order to promote more efficient allocation and use of productive resources by relying on market mechanisms instead government decree.
- Devaluing the currency in order to make exports more competitive, thus resulting in more dollars to service the foreign debt.
- Cutting or constraining wages and eliminating or weakening mechanisms protecting labour such as the minimum wage to remove what were seen as artificial barriers to the mobility of local and foreign capital.

By the late 1980s, with over seventy Third World countries submitting to IMF and World Bank programmes, stabilization, structural adjustment and shock therapy managed from distant Washington became the common condition of the South. While structural adjustment was justified as necessary to create the conditions that would enable Third World countries to repay their debts to Northern banks, there was a more strategic objective: to dismantle the system of state-assisted capitalism that served as the domestic base for the national capitalist elites. In 1988, a survey of structural adjustment programmes (SAPs) carried out by the UN Commission for Africa concluded that the essence of SAPs was the 'reduction/removal of direct state intervention in the productive and redistributive sectors of the economy'.[18]

As for Latin America, one analyst noted that the USA took advantage of 'this period of financial strain to insist that debtor countries remove the government from the economy as the price of getting credit'.[19] Similarly, a retrospective look at the decade of adjustment in a book published by the Inter-American Development Bank in 1992 identified the removal of the state from economic activity as the centrepiece of the ideological perspective that guided the structural reforms of the 1980s.

By the end of the twelve-year-long Reagan–Bush era in 1992, the South had been transformed: from Argentina to Ghana, state participation in the economy had been drastically curtailed; government enterprises were passing into private hands in the name of efficiency; protectionist barriers to Northern imports were being radically reduced; and, through export-first policies, the internal economy was more tightly integrated into the Northern-dominated capitalist world markets.

Taming the Tigers There was one area of the South relatively untouched by the first phase of the Northern economic counter-revolution: East and Southeast Asia. Here practically all the economic systems displayed the same features of state-assisted capitalism found elsewhere in the South: an activist government intervening in key areas of the economy, a focus on industrialization in order to escape the fate of being simply agricultural or raw material producers, protection of the domestic market from foreign competition, and tight controls on foreign investment.

Where the key East and Southeast Asian economies appeared to differ from other economies in the South was mainly in the presence of a fairly strong state that was able to discipline local elites, the greater internalization of a developmentalist direction by the state elite, and the pursuit of aggressive mercantilist policies aimed at gaining markets in First World countries, particularly the United States.

The front-line status in Asia of many of these so-called 'newly industrializing countries' (NICs) during the Cold War ensured that Washington would turn a blind eye to many of their deviations from the free market ideal. But as the Cold War wound down from the mid-1980s, the USA began to redefine its economic policy towards East Asia as the creation of a 'level playing field' for its corporations via liberalization, deregulation and more extensive privatization of Asian economies.

It was a goal that Washington pursued by various means in the late 1980s and early 1990s. Japanese capital, however, was relocating many of its industrial operations to East and Southeast Asia to offset the loss of competitiveness in Japan caused by the rapid appreciation of the yen triggered by the Plaza Accord in 1985. Access to this capital allowed countries such as South Korea, Thailand and Indonesia to ignore the requirements of formal structural adjustment programmes that were foisted on them by the World Bank and the IMF in the early 1980s when they were temporarily destabilized by the debt crisis.

In its effort to discipline the NICs, the USA resorted to both multilateral and unilateral mechanisms. While Republican administrations of Reagan and Bush Senior preferred the unilateralist approach, the Clinton administration, at least in the beginning, appeared to favour a multilateralist solution such as pushing the Asia Pacific Cooperation (APEC) as the framework for disciplining the Asian economies.

A brief look at the dynamics of APEC is worthwhile, for the rise and fall of this body illustrates the limits of US power in the pre-financial crisis period.

Japan had initially proposed the formation of APEC as a consultative body along the lines of the Organisation for Economic Co-operation and Development (OECD). In the early 1990s, however, Australia and the USA sought to move APEC from being a loose grouping to becoming a free trade area in which countries would commit themselves to pursue mandated national plans for comprehensive liberalization with specified time lines that would end with regional free trade. Washington's idea was to make APEC the equivalent of a trans-Pacific NAFTA (North American Free Trade Agreement).

The high points of this effort were the Seattle Summit in 1993, when the USA took the leadership for an APEC free trade area from Australia, and the Bogor, Indonesia, Summit in 1994, when the date 2020 was set as the time that the region would achieve free trade, defined as a condition where all tariffs would be brought down to 0 to 5 per cent.

The Asian response to this initiative was to agree rhetorically to the goal of regional free trade but to stymie it in practice by saying that liberalization should be voluntary and that its pace should be adjusted to the particular situation of each country.

The underlying dynamics of the struggle within APEC were perhaps best captured by an Australian economic journalist, Kenneth Davidson:

> The unstated Anglo-Saxon assumption behind APEC is that if the Anglo-Saxon countries can persuade Asian countries to play the economic development game according to Anglo-Saxon rules, the game will be transformed into a neoclassical, laissez faire, positive-sum game in which the players will be transmuted from countries or tribes into firms and individuals.[20]

Managed capitalism of the Asian variety, he continued, was proving, however, 'more resistant to cultural and political convergence imposed by globalizing forces', and the Australian-American goal at APEC was 'to try to get the Asian winners of the economic game to deny the cultural basis of their success in order to create the conditions whereby the losers can become winners'.[21]

At the Osaka Summit in 1995, under the leadership of the host, Japan, the Asian bloc managed to torpedo the US 2020 plan by extracting a final declaration that liberalization would be voluntary. After Osaka, the USA abandoned its effort to make APEC like NAFTA, and the Clinton administration was left with unilateralism in trade and financial diplomacy as the principal weapon to deploy against the Asian NICs.

Unilateralism was aggressively pursued, sometimes to the point of *de facto* trade war. Washington's mood was aptly captured by a senior US official who told a capital markets conference in San Francisco that 'Although the NICs may be regarded as tigers because they are strong, ferocious traders, the analogy has a darker side. Tigers live in the jungle, and by the law of the jungle. They are a shrinking population.'[22]

With some assistance from the IMF and the World Bank, unilateral pressure succeeded in getting key Asian countries to liberalize their capital accounts and to move to greater liberalization of their financial sectors. But when it came to trade liberalization, the results were meagre, except perhaps in the case of Korea, whose trade surplus with the USA had been turned into a trade deficit by the early 1980s. However, even this development did not change the US trade representative's assessment of Korea as 'one of the toughest places in the world to do business'.[23] As for the Southeast Asian countries, Washington's assessment was that while they might have liberalized their capital accounts and financial sectors, they remained highly protected when it came to trade and were dangerously flirting with 'trade-distorting' exercises in industrial policy, such as Malaysia's national car project, the Proton Saga, or Indonesia's drive to set up a passenger aircraft industry.

The indiscriminate financial liberalization demanded by Washington and the Bretton Woods institutions, coupled with the high interest rate and fixed currency regime favoured by local financial authorities, brought massive amounts of foreign capital into the region. But it also served as the wide highway through which $100 billion exited in 1997 in a massive stampede in response to dislocations caused by over-investment and unrestricted capital inflows, such as the collapse of the real-estate market and widening current account deficits.

A golden opportunity to push the US agenda opened up with the financial crisis, and Washington did not hesitate to exploit it to the hilt, advancing its interests behind the banner of free market reform. Chalmers Johnson has asserted that a good case can be made that Washington's opportunistic behaviour during the Asian financial crisis reflected the fact that 'having defeated the fascists and the communists, the United States now sought to defeat its last remaining rivals for global dominance: the nations of East Asia that had used the conditions of the Cold War to enrich themselves'.[24] A close look at the stabilization programmes imposed by the IMF on the key countries of Indonesia, Thailand and Indonesia indeed reveals that the rollback of protectionism and activist state intervention were strategically incorporated into them. These programmes went beyond mere stabilization and short-term adjustment, leading credence to claims that in the critical years of 1998 and 1999, the USA was interested not in the economic recovery of the Asian tigers but in their resubordination.

In Thailand, local authorities agreed to remove all limitations on foreign ownership of Thai financial firms, accelerate the privatization of state enterprises and revise bankruptcy laws along lines demanded by the country's foreign creditors. As the US trade representative told Congress, the Thai government's 'commitments to restructure public enterprises and accelerate privatization of certain key sectors – including energy, transportation, utilities, and communications – which will enhance market-driven competition and deregulation – [are expected] to create new business opportunities for US firms'.[25]

In Indonesia, the US trade representative emphasized that

the IMF's conditions for granting a massive stabilization package addressed practices that have long been the subject of this [Clinton] Administration's bilateral trade policy ... Most notable in this respect is the commitment by Indonesia to eliminate the tax, tariff, and credit privileges provided to the national car project. Additionally, the IMF program seeks broad reform of Indonesian trade and investment policy, like the aircraft project, monopolies and domestic trade restrictive practices, that stifle competition by limiting access for foreign goods and services.[26]

The national car project and the plan to set up a passenger jet aircraft industry were efforts at industrial policy that had elicited the strong disapproval of Detroit and Boeing, respectively.

In the case of Korea, the US Treasury and the IMF did not conceal their close working relationship, with the Fund clearly in a subordinate position. Not surprisingly, the concessions made by the Koreans – including raising the limit on foreign ownership of corporate stocks to 55 per cent, permitting the establishment of foreign financial institutions, full liberalization of the financial and capital market, abolition of the car classification system, and agreement to end government-directed lending for industrial policy goals – had a one-to-one correspondence with US bilateral policy towards Korea before the crisis. As the US trade representative candidly told US congressmen:

Policy-driven, rather than market-driven economic activity, meant that US industry encountered many specific structural barriers to trade, investment, and competition in Korea. For example, Korea maintained restrictions on foreign ownership and operations, and had a list of market access impediments ... The Korea stabilization package, negotiated with the IMF in December 1997, should help open and expand competition in Korea by creating a more market-driven economy ... [I]f it continues on the path to reform there will be important benefits not only for Korea but also the United States.[27]

Summing up Washington's strategic goal, Jeff Garten, under-secretary of commerce during President Bill Clinton's first term, said, 'Most of these countries are going through a dark and deep tunnel … But on the other end there is going to be a significantly different Asia in which American firms have achieved a much deeper market penetration, much greater access'.[28]

By 1998, transnationals and US financial firms were buying up Asian assets from Seoul to Bangkok at fire sale prices.

Dismantling the UN development system   This assault on the NICs via the IMF stabilization programmes and on the broader South via Bretton Woods-imposed structural adjustment was accompanied by a major effort to emasculate the United Nations as a vehicle for the Southern agenda. Wielding the power of the purse, the United States, whose contribution funds some 20–25 per cent of the UN budget, moved to silence NIEO rhetoric in all the key UN institutions dealing with the North–South divide: the Economic and Social Council (ECOSOC), the UN Development Program, and the General Assembly. US pressure resulted as well in the effective dismantling of the UN Center on Transnational Corporations (TNCs), whose high-quality work in tracking the activities of the TNCs in the South, had earned the ire of the TNCs. Also abolished was the post of director general for international economic co-operation and development, which 'had been one of the few concrete outcomes, and certainly the most noteworthy, of the efforts of the developing countries during the NIEO negotiations to secure a stronger UN presence in support of international economic cooperation and development'.[28]

But the focus of the Northern counter-offensive was the defanging, if not dismantling of UNCTAD. After giving in to the South during the UNCTAD IV negotiations in Nairobi in 1976 by agreeing to the creation of the commodity stabilization scheme known as the Integrated Program for Commodities, the North, during UNCTAD V in Belgrade, refused the South's programme of debt cancellation and other measures intended to revive Third World economies and thus contribute to global recovery at a time of worldwide recession.[30] The Northern offensive escalated during UNCTAD VIII, held in Cartagena in 1992. At this watershed meeting, the North successfully opposed all linkages of UNCTAD discussions with the Uruguay Round negotiations of the GATT and managed to erode UNCTAD's negotiation functions, thus calling its existence into question.[31] UNCTAD's main function would henceforth be limited to 'analysis, consensus building on some trade-related issues, and technical assistance'.[32]

The World Trade Organization: Third Pillar of the System

UNCTAD continues to survive, but the truth of the matter is that it has been rendered impotent by the WTO, which came into being following the signing of the Marrakesh Accord in April 1994, which put in force the agreements concluded during the eight-year Uruguay Round of the General Agreement on Tariffs and Trade (GATT). The WTO was forty-six years late in coming into being, although it had initially been regarded by liberal internationalists in the USA and Britain as the third pillar of the Bretton Woods system, doing for trade what the IMF did for finance and the World Bank for economic reconstruction. A global trading organization had initially been scheduled to come into existence as the International Trade Organization (ITO) in 1948, but the threat of non-ratification by unilateralist forces in the US Senate led to its being shelved in favour of the much weaker GATT by the defensive Truman administration.

By the mid-1980s, trade rivalries with Europe and Japan, rising import penetration of the US market by Third World countries, frustration at the inability of US goods to enter Southern markets, and the rise of new competitors in the shape of the East Asian NICs made the US the leading advocate of a much-expanded GATT with real coercive teeth. Central to the founding of the

WTO were the twin drives of managing the trade rivalry among the leading industrial countries while containing the threat posed by the South to the prevailing global economic structure.

In this sense, the WTO must be seen as a continuation or extension of the same Northern reaction that drove structural adjustment. While its emergence consolidated the structural hegemony of the North as a whole, it served the interests of the world's prime economic power in particular. This becomes clear once we examine the circumstances that surrounded its creation.

World trade did not need the WTO to expand seventeen-fold between 1948 and 1997, from $124 billion to $10,772 billion.[33] This expansion took place under the flexible General Agreement on Trade and Tariffs (GATT) trade regime. The founding of the WTO in 1995 did not respond to a collapse or crisis of world trade such as happened in the 1930s. It was not necessary for global peace, since no world war or trade-related war had taken place during that period. In the seven major interstate wars that took place in that period – the Korean War of 1950–53, the Vietnam War of 1945–75, the Suez Crisis of 1956, the 1967 Arab–Israeli War, the 1973 Arab–Israeli War, the 1982 Falklands War and the Gulf War of 1990 – trade conflict did not figure even remotely as a cause.

GATT was, in fact, functioning reasonably well as a framework for liberalizing world trade. Its dispute settlement system was flexible, and its recognition of the 'special and differential status' of developing countries provided the space in a global economy for Third World countries to use trade policy for development and industrialization.

Why was the WTO established following the Uruguay Round of 1986–94? Of the major trading powers, Japan was very ambivalent, concerned as it was to protect its agriculture as well as its particular system of industrial production that, through formal and informal mechanisms, gave its local producers primary right to exploit the domestic market. The European Union (EU), well on the way to becoming a self-sufficient trading bloc, was likewise ambivalent, knowing that its highly subsidized system in agriculture would come under attack. Though demanding greater access to their manufactured and agricultural products in the Northern economies, the developing countries did not see this as being accomplished through a comprehensive agreement enforced by a powerful trade bureaucracy, but through discrete negotiations and agreements in the model of the integrated programme for commodities (IPCs) and commodity stabilization fund agreed upon under the aegis of the UN Conference on Trade and Development (UNCTAD) in the late 1970s.

The founding of the WTO primarily served the interests of the United States. Just as it was the USA which blocked the founding of the International Trade Organization (ITO) in 1948, when it felt that this would not serve its position of overwhelming economic dominance in the post-war world, so it was that the USA became the dominant lobbyist for the comprehensive Uruguay Round and the founding of the WTO in the late 1980s and early 1990s, when it felt that more competitive global conditions had created a situation where its corporate interests now demanded an opposite stance.

Just as it was the United States' threat in the 1950s to leave GATT if it was not allowed to maintain protective mechanisms for milk and other agricultural products that led to agricultural trade's exemption from GATT rules, it was US pressure that brought agriculture into the GATT–WTO system in 1995. And the reason for Washington's change of mind was articulated quite candidly by then US agriculture secretary John Block at the start of the Uruguay Round negotiations in 1986: '[The] idea that developing countries should feed themselves is an anachronism from a bygone era. They could better ensure their food security by relying on US agricultural products, which are available, in most cases at much lower cost.'[34] Washington, of course, did not just have developing country markets in mind, but also Japan, South Korea and the EU.

It was the USA that mainly pushed to bring services under the

WTO coverage, with its assessment that in the new burgeoning area of international services, and particularly in financial services, its corporations had a lead that needed to be preserved. It was also the USA that pushed to expand WTO jurisdiction to the so-called 'trade-related investment measures' (TRIMs) and 'trade-related intellectual property rights' (TRIPs). The first sought to eliminate barriers to the system of internal cross-border trade of product components among TNC (transnational corporation) subsidiaries that had been imposed by developing countries in order to develop their industries; the second to consolidate the US advantage in the cutting-edge knowledge-intensive industries.

It was the USA that forced the creation of the WTO's formidable dispute-resolution and enforcement mechanism after being frustrated with what US trade officials considered weak GATT efforts to enforce rulings favourable to the US. As Washington's academic point man on trade, C. Fred Bergsten, head of the Institute of International Economics, told the US Senate, the strong WTO dispute settlement mechanism serves American interests because 'we can now use the full weight of the international machinery to go after those trade barriers, reduce them, get them eliminated'.[35]

In sum, it has been Washington's changing perception of the needs of its economic interest groups that has shaped and reshaped the international trading regime. It was not global necessity that gave birth to the WTO in 1995. It was the United States' assessment that the interests of its corporations were no longer served by a loose and flexible GATT but needed an all-powerful and wide-ranging WTO. From the free market paradigm that underpins it, to the rules and regulations set forth in the different agreements that make up the Uruguay Round, to its system of decision-making and accountability, the WTO was regarded even by many Europeans and Japanese as a blueprint for the global hegemony of corporate America. It sought to institutionalize the accumulated advantages of US corporations.

The Group of Seven: An International Directorate?

The Bretton Woods institutions and the GATT–WTO provided a comprehensive structure of multilateral control over the global economy by the rich countries led by the United States. But the creation of 'consensus' among the dominant powers was a function that was not performed adequately by the three institutions, where the highest national representatives were people much below ministerial rank in their respective national bureaucracies. It was the need for a central institution to provide broad strategic and policy agreement among them that caused the institution known as the Group of Seven (G-7) to come into being. Started during a rather small summit of the world's leading industrial economies in Rambouillet, France, in 1975, the G-7 – now the G-8, with the inclusion of post-Soviet Russia – has evolved into what one report called 'the nearest the world comes to having an apex body concerned with the global economy'.[36]

The annual summit was the high point of the G-7 process, and over the years, the event became a highly elaborate affair attended by government delegations that numbered in the thousands.[37] While the summit of heads of state drew the most media attention, perhaps equally critical in terms of working out joint strategies was the meeting of finance ministers that took place a few days before the summit. Apart from these two sessions, there was 'quiet bureaucratic coordination throughout the year'.[38]

In its first few years, the G-8 evolved mainly as a forum for discussing and loosely co-ordinating the macroeconomic policies of the rich countries in order to navigate a direction of stable growth that would avoid the Scylla of high inflation on the one side and the Charybdis of deep recession on the other. It was credited with a number of successes in the pursuit of this goal, including preventing the 1987 stock exchange crash from triggering global deflation by co-ordinating the monetary policies of the advanced countries.[39]

Even in its heyday, however, the G–7 was criticized as having little to offer the developing world. As one analyst put it,

> the issues that the G7 normally considers fall within a narrow range of macroeconomic management, particularly in the monetary and financial fields. It neither considers nor takes a far-reaching decisions on some of the most urgent problems confronting the global community: for example, population growth, environmental degradation, drug trafficking, flow of refugees, food security, child survival, women's empowerment, human development.[40]

It was, however, the blatant exclusiveness and non-representativeness of the G–7 that drew the sharpest criticism, even from liberal quarters. As the Commission on Global Governance put it, the G–7:

> represents only 12 per cent of the world's population. By excluding China and India, it can no longer even claim to represent the world's major economies. The development issues that concern most of humanity have low priority on its agenda. Looking decades ahead, it will become more and more anachronistic that non–OECD economies that account for a large and growing slice of the world economy are not represented in the main body with an overview of international economic issues.[41]

Notes

1. World Trade Organization, *The Results of the Uruguay Round of Multilateral Trade Negotiations: The Legal Texts* (Geneva: WTO, 1994), p. 557.

2. See, among other works, *Towards a New Trade Policy for Development* (New York: UNCTAD, 1964).

3. Bernard Nossiter, *The Global Struggle for More* (New York: Harper and Row, 1987), pp. 42–3.

4. Ibid., p. 45.

5. Nassau Adams, 'The UN's Neglected Brief –the Advancement of All Peoples', in Erskine Childers (ed.), *Challenges to the UN* (New York: St. Martins Press), p. 31.

6. Nossiter, p. 34.

7. Ibid., p. 35.

8. Adams, p. 31.

9. Alfred Maizels, 'Reforming the World Commodity Economy', in Michael Cutajar (ed.), *UNCTAD and the North–South Dialogue* (New York: Pergamon Press, 1985), p. 108; United Nations, *World Economic Survey* (New York: United Nations, 1988), p. 42.

10. Karin Lissakers, *Banks, Borrowers, and the Establishment* (New York: Basic Books, 1991), p. 56.

11. Eduardo White, 'The Question of Foreign Investments and the Economic Crisis of Latin America', in Richard Feinberg and Ricardo Ffrench-Davis (eds), *Development and External Debt in Latin America: Bases for a New Consensus* (Notre Dame, IN: University of Notre Dame Press, 1988), pp. 157–8.

12. Lissakers, p. 56.

13. White, p. 158.

14. Quoted in Nossiter, p. 57.

15. Doug Bandow, 'The US Role in Promoting Third World Development', in Heritage Foundation, *US Aid to the Developing World: A Free Market Agenda* (Washington, DC: Heritage Foundation, 1985), p. xxii.

16. Ibid., p. xxiv.

17. Ibid., pp. xxiii–xxiv.

18. Cited in Seamus Cleary, 'Toward a New Adjustment in Africa', in 'Beyond Adjustment', special issue of *African Environment*, Vol. 7, Nos 1–4, p. 357.

19. John Sheahan, 'Development Dichotomies and Economic Development Strategy', in Simon Teitel (ed.), *Toward a New Development Strategy for Latin America* (Washington, DC: Inter-American Development Bank, 1992), p. 53.

20. Kenneth Davidson, 'Hard Lessons Ahead as We Learn to Deal with Asia', *The Age*, November 15, 1994, p. 19.

21. Ibid.

22. David Mulford, 'Remarks before the Asia-Pacific Capital Markets Conference', San Francisco, November 17, 1987.

23. Testimony of Ambassador Charlene Barshefsky, US Trade Representative, before the House Ways and Means Trade Subcommittee, US Congress, February 24, 1998.

24. Chalmers Johnson, *Blowback: The Costs and Consequences of American Empire* (New York: Henry Holt, 2000), p. 206.

25. Ibid.

26. Ibid.

27. Ibid.

28. Quoted in 'Worsening Financial Flu Lowers Immunity to US Business', *New York Times*, February 1, 1998.

29. Adam's 'The UN's Neglected Brief', p. 43.

30. South Commission, *The Challenge to the South* (New York: Oxford University Press, 1991), p. 217.

31. Myriam van der Stichele, 'World Trade – Free Trade for Whom, Fair for Whom?', in Childers (ed.), *Challenges to the UN*, p. 69.

32. 'South Decries Move to Close UNCTAD, UNIDO', *Third World Resurgence*, No. 56, p. 41.

33. Figures from World Trade Organization, *Annual Report 1998: International Trade Statistics* (Geneva: WTO, 1998), p. 12.

34. Quoted in 'Cakes and Caviar: The Dunkel Draft and Third World Agriculture', *Ecologist*, Vol. 23, No. 6 (November–December 1993), p. 220.

35. C. Fred Bergsten, director, Institute of International Economics, testimony before US Senate, Washington, DC, October 13, 1994.

36. Commission on Global Governance, *Our Global Neighborhood* (Oxford: Oxford University Press, 1995), p. 154.

37. *Financial Times,* July 23, 2001.

38. Mahbub ul Haq, 'The Case for an Economic Security Council', in Albert Pasolini et al., *Between Sovereignty and Global Governance* (New York: St. Martins Press, 1998), p. 230.

39. Commission on Global Governance, p. 154.

40. Mahbub ul Haq.

41. Commission on Global Governance.

THREE

Sidestepping Democracy at the Multilateral Agencies

If the developing countries have been disadvantaged by the policies of the Bretton Woods institutions and the World Trade Organization, a great part of the reason is that they have been marginalized in the formal decision-making systems of these institutions. An analysis of global economic governance would not be complete without a discussion of these structures, if only to show what global economic governance should not be like.

The World Bank

A US Treasury Department report in the early 1980s captured the dominance exercised by the United States in the World Bank in particular:

> The United States was instrumental in shaping the structure and mission of the World Bank along Western, market-oriented lines ... We were also responsible ... for the emergence of a corporate entity with a weighted voting run by a board of directors, headed by a high-caliber American-dominated management, and well-qualified professional staff. As a charter member and major shareholder in the World Bank, the United States secured the sole right to a permanent seat on the Bank's Board of Directors.[1]

Formal decision-making power is based on the size of capital subscriptions. While significantly below the 42 per cent share of voting power that it had at the time the Bank began operations in 1946, the 17.6 per cent it currently possesses is above the critical 15 per cent it needs to retain a veto over major lending decisions. The USA has jealously guarded its pre-eminent shareholder role. Although Japan has been pressing for a larger share, the USA has been able to limit its capital share and voting power to 8 per cent.

Formal power is supplemented by informal mechanisms. By 'tradition', the Bank's president is always an American citizen appointed by the US government, and the Bank's location in Washington, DC, gives the US Treasury Department easy access to it and helps ensure that US citizens account for one-quarter of senior management and the higher-level professional staff.[2]

Formal and informal mechanisms ensure a situation where '[o]ther significant actors – management, major donors, and major recipients – have recognized the United States as a major voice in the [multilateral development] banks. They know from past experience that we are capable and willing to pursue important policy objectives in the banks by exercising the financial and political leverage at our disposal.'[3] In a study of fourteen of 'the most significant issues' that sparked debate at the Bank – ranging from blocking observer status for the Palestine Liberation Organization (PLO) to halting Bank aid to Vietnam and Afghanistan – the United States was able to impose its view as Bank policy in twelve cases.[4]

The World Bank has been an important arm of US global policy, in the view of the Treasury Department. Indeed, 'Neither bilateral assistance nor private sector flows, if available, are as effective in influencing LDC [less developed countries] as the MDB's [multilateral development banks].'[5] As a Congressional Research Service analysis put it, the advantage of the World Bank and multilateral development banks from a US point of view was that they 'perform the difficult task of requiring performance standards of their borrowers, a task which the United States and other lenders may be reluctant to impose on a bilateral basis'.[6] A case in point was cited by former Deputy Treasury Secretary

Peter McPherson, who observed with respect to the Philippines: 'We have not been particularly successful ourselves in winning policy reforms from the Philippines. Because it is something of a disinterested party, however, the World Bank has been enormously successful in negotiating important policy changes which we strongly support.'[7]

The International Monetary Fund

As in the case with the World Bank, the developed economies dominate the International Monetary Fund (IMF), with the five largest economies having 45.47 per cent of the total votes in the Board of Governors, the USA being pre-eminent with 19 per cent. Since other rich countries have 21.42 per cent of the votes, the developed countries as a group have the voting power to block all decisions requiring majorities. In response to pressure from developing countries' demand to have a larger say in decision-making, the developed countries pushed through the Second Amendment to the Articles of Agreement. This detailed fifty-three different decisions requiring supermajorities of 70 to 85 per cent to be passed, which meant that subgroups of 'the developed have the ability to block decisions requiring 70 to 85 per cent majorities'.[8]

The special weight of the USA, in particular, has been carefully protected through the creation of new rules – a process detailed in an important article by Richard Leaver and Leonard Seabrooke. By the early 1970s, the USA's voting power had declined from 30 per cent and was fast approaching the 20 per cent threshold protecting 'special decisions'. Japan and other countries were, however, seeking a change in voting power to reflect their greater weight in the world economy. This was, however, something that 'Washington would not tolerate'.

It stonewalled a review of the Fund's quotas, drawing out the process. But in the end a deal was struck with the Japanese and the Europeans. The voting power of the US was indeed reduced to 19 per cent, but the supermajority requirement for 'special decisions' was racheted up to 85 per cent. This extraordinary double movement provided the precedent for a similar deal inside the World Bank a decade later, so setting one of the major parameters of the distribution of political power governing the Fund through the period of the Latin and Asian debt crisis.[9]

Democracy is also ill served by the fact that the Fund is extremely non-transparent, since despite the fact that members have voting rights, a formal vote, either in the Board of Executive Directors or in the Board of Governors, is 'a relatively rare occurrence'.[10] The US executive director for the greater part of the Clinton administration, for instance, revealed that the executive board actually had votes on approximately a dozen out of 2,000 decisions during her tenure. Instead, most decisions are made instead by a form of consensus.

However, as Ngaire Wood has noted, consensus as practised by the Fund has non-democratic implications. One is that it merely serves to cover up the unequal power relations that would reveal themselves were a formal vote taken, since 'formal powers have an underlying force of which all participants in meetings are aware'.[11] Another is that 'states and NGOs that are not present during the proceedings find it very hard to figure out what actually transpired, thus undermining transparency and accountability'.[12]

Although the Fund is by tradition headed by a European, it is extraordinarily submissive towards the US Treasury Department. During the Fund bail-outs of Mexico in 1994–95 and Southeast Asian countries in 1997, IMF Managing Director Michel Camdessus was widely regarded as being micromanaged by Secretary of the Treasury Robert Rubin and his key aide Larry Summers, provoking the *New York Times* to call the Fund 'a proxy for the United States'.[13]

The Fund's special functions for Washington were what led the latter to veto the creation of the Asian Monetary Fund (AMF) proposed by Japan during the IMF–World Bank meeting in Hong Kong in September 1997. As analyst Eric Altbach claims, Washington's vehement response stemmed from the fact that increasing congressional constraints on the president's power to commit US bilateral funds to international initiatives made the USA 'more dependent on its power in the IMF to exercise influence on financial matters in Asia. In this context, an Asian monetary fund in which Japan was a major player would be a blow to the US role in the region.' [14]

The World Trade Organization

One of the key reasons for the collapse of the World Trade Organization Ministerial in Seattle in December 1999 was the absence of transparent decision-making. Stories abounded of ministers from developing countries complaining of being lost at the Seattle Convention Center, looking for a 'Green Room' where key decisions would be made, not knowing that the Green Room referred not to a real room at the convention centre but to an exclusive process of decision-making.

During the WTO ratification process in 1994, partisans of the new trade organization portrayed it as a one-country-one-vote organization where the United States would actually have the same vote as Rwanda. In truth, the WTO is not governed democratically via a one-country-one-vote system like UN General Assembly or through a system of weighted voting like the World Bank or the IMF. While, according to its constitution, it is a one-country-one-vote system, 'consensus' is the process that reigns in the World Trade Organization, one that it took over from the old GATT, where the last time a vote was taken was in 1959.

Consensus, in practice, is a process whereby the big trading countries impose their consensus on the less powerful countries. As C. Fred Bergsten, a prominent partisan of globalization who heads the Institute of International Economics, put it during US Senate hearings on the ratification of the GATT–WTO Agreement in 1994, the WTO 'does not work by voting. It works by a consensus arrangement which, to tell the truth, is managed by four – the Quads: the United States, Japan, European Union, and Canada ... Those countries have to agree if any major steps are going to be made. But no votes.'[15]

Though the Ministerial and the General Council are theoretically the highest decision-making bodies of the WTO, decisions are arrived at not in formal plenaries but in non-transparent backroom sessions known as the 'Green Room', after the colour of the Director General's room at the WTO headquarters in Geneva. With surprising frankness, at a press conference in Seattle, shortly after the ministerial collapse, the US Trade Representative Charlene Barshefsky described the dynamics and consequences of the Green Room:

> The process, including even at Singapore as recently as three years ago, was a rather exclusionary one. All the meetings were held between 20 and 30 key countries...And this meant 100 countries, 100, were never in the room...[T]his led to extraordinarily bad feeling that they were left out of the process and that the results even at Singapore had been dictated to them by the 25 to 30 countries who were in the room.[16]

Barshefsky admitted that 'the WTO has outgrown the processes appropriate to an earlier time. An increasing and necessary view, generally shared among the members, was that we needed a process which had a greater degree of internal transparency and inclusion to accommodate a larger and more diverse membership.' This was backed up by UK Secretary of State Stephen Byers, who stated that the 'WTO will not be able to continue in its present form. There has to be fundamental and radical change in order for it to meet the needs and aspirations of all 134 of its members.'[17]

Accepted previously as unavoidable by many governments and peoples in the South, the decision-making structures of the multilateral agencies were devoid of democratic legitimacy by the end of the twentieth century. This was not sustainable.

Notes

1. US Treasury Department, *Assessment of US Participation in the Multilateral Development Banks in the 1980s* (Washington, DC: US Treasury Department, 1982), chapter 3, p. 1.

2. Richard Feinberg, 'An Open Letter to the World Bank's New President', in Richard Feinberg et al. (eds), *Between Two Worlds: The World Bank's Next Decade* (New Brunswick, NJ: Transaction Books, 1986), p. 2.

3. *US Treasury Department*, Chapter 3, p. 2.

4. Ibid., Chapter 3.

5. Ibid., Chapter 2, p. 18.

6. Congressional Research Service, *The United States and the Multilateral Development Banks* (Washington, DC: US Government Printing Office, 1974), p. 5.

7. Quoted in Walden Bello, 'The Role of the World Bank in US Foreign Policy' *Covert Action Information Quarterly*, No. 5 (Fall 1990), p. 22.

8. Joseph Gold, cited in Mark Zacher, 'Redesigning the International Financial Architecture: Voting Power and Power Sharing in the IMF', paper delivered at the Conference on the International Financial Architecture,' Center for Global Studies, University of Victoria, British Columbia, August 29–30, 2001.

9. Richard Leaver and Leonard Seabrooke, 'Can the IMF be Reformed?', in Walden Bello et al. (eds), *Global Finance* (London: Zed Books, 2000), p. 102.

10. Zamora, quoted in Zacher, p. 126.

11. Ngaire Wood, quoted in Zacher, p. 127.

12. Ibid., p. 126.

13. Cited in '20 Questions on the IMF', *Multinational Monitor*, April 2000, p. 23.

14. Eric Altbach, 'The Asian Monetary Fund Proposal: A Case Study of Japanese Regional Leadership', *Japanese Economic Institute Report*, No. 477A, 1997, pp. 8–9.

15. Testimony before the US Senate Committee on Commerce, Science, and Technology, Washington, DC, October 13, 1994.

16. Press briefing, Seattle, Washington, December 2, 1999.

17. Quoted in 'Deadline Set for WTO Reforms', *Guardian News Service*, January 10, 2000.

FOUR
The Crisis of Legitimacy

With the founding of the WTO, neoliberalism or, as it was more grandiosely styled, the 'Washington Consensus', seem to have carried all before it by the mid-1990s. As one of its key partisans later remarked, in a nostalgic vein, 'the Washington Consensus seemed to gain near-universal approval and provided a guiding ideology and underlying intellectual consensus for the world economy, which was quite new in modern history'.[1] Less than five years later, the Consensus was in tatters and the key institutions of global governance that underpinned it were experiencing a severe crisis of legitimacy.

The IMF's Stalingrad

If any event may be said to have contributed to undermining the Fund, it was the Asian financial crisis, whose legacy of collapsed financial systems, bankrupt corporations and rising poverty and inequality continue to plague the region. One can say that the Asian financial crisis was the Stalingrad of the IMF. Bearing in mind the limits of metaphor, the IMF during the Asian financial crisis acted like the German Sixth Army, making one wrong move after another on the way to disaster.

It was the IMF that helped trigger the massive flow of volatile speculative capital into the region by pressing the Asian governments for capital account liberalization prior to the crisis, egged on itself by the US Treasury Department. It was the IMF that confidently moved in after the panicky flight of speculative capital began, with a tight fiscal and monetary formula that, by drastically reducing government's capacity to act as counter-force to the downturn in private sector activity, converted the financial crisis into an economic collapse.

It was the IMF that assembled the high-profile multi-billion-dollar rescue packages that were meant to rescue foreign creditors, even as local banks, finance companies, and corporations were told to bite the bullet by accepting bankruptcy. It was the IMF that imposed on the fallen economies a programme of radical deregulation and financial and trade liberalization that was essentially Washington's pre-crisis agenda the tigers had been able to frustrate during their days of prosperity. And it was the IMF that, at the urging of the US Treasury Department, killed the proposal for an Asian Monetary Fund (AMF), which would have pooled together the reserves from the more financially sound economies to serve as a fund from which those subjected to speculative attack could draw to shore up their currencies.

As the stricken economies registered negative growth rates and record unemployment rates in 1998, and over 1 million people in Thailand and 21 million in Indonesia fell below the poverty line, the IMF not surprisingly joined corrupt governments, banks and George Soros as the villains of the piece in the view of millions of newly impoverished Koreans, Thais and Indonesians.

But equally as significant for its future as an institution was the fact that the IMF's actions brought the long-simmering conflict over the role of the Fund within the US elite to a boil. The American right denounced the Fund for promoting moral hazard, with some personalities such as former US Treasury Secretary George Shultz calling for its abolition, while orthodox liberals such as Jeffrey Sachs and Jagdish Bhagwati attacked the Fund for being a threat to global macroeconomic stability and prosperity. Late in 1998, a conservative–liberal alliance in the US Congress came within a hair's breath of denying the IMF a $14.5 billion increase in the US quota. The quota increase was salvaged, with arm-twisting on the part of the Clinton administration, but it was clear that the long-time internationalist consensus within the US elite that had propped up the Fund for over five decades was unravelling.

The Past Catches Up

The Fund's performance during the Asian financial crisis led to a widespread reappraisal of the Fund's role in the Third World in the 1980s and early 1990s, when structural adjustment programmes were imposed over ninety developing and transition economies.

Judged by the extremely narrow criterion of promoting growth, structural adjustment programmes were a failure, with a number of studies showing that adjustment had brought about a negative effect on growth. After over fifteen years, it was hard to point to more than a handful as having brought about stable growth, among them the very questionable case of Pinochet's Chile. What structural adjustment had done instead was to institutionalize stagnation in Africa, Latin America and other parts of the Third World. A study by the Center for Economic and Policy Research shows that 77 per cent of countries for which data are available saw their per capita rate of growth fall significantly from the period 1960–80 to the period 1980–2000, the structural adjustment period. In Latin America, income expanded by 75 per cent during the 1960s and 1970s, when the region's economies were relatively closed, but grew by only 6 per cent in the past two decades.[2] Average incomes in sub-Saharan Africa and the old Eastern bloc have actually contracted.'[3]

Broadening the criteria of success to include reduction of inequality and bringing down poverty, the results were unquestionable – structural adjustment was a blight on the Third World. A study by Mattias Lundberg and Lyn Squire of the World Bank summed it up thus: 'the poor are far more vulnerable to shifts in relative international prices, and this vulnerability is magnified by the country's openness to trade … [A]t least in the short term, globalization appears to increase both poverty and inequality.'[4] The number of people globally living in poverty – that is, on less than a dollar a day – increased from 1.1 billion in 1985 to 1.2 billion in 1998, and was expected to reach 1.3 billion by 2000. According to a recent World Bank study, the absolute number of people living in poverty rose in the 1990s in Eastern Europe, South Asia, Latin America and the Caribbean, and sub-Saharan Africa – all areas that came under the sway of structural adjustment programmes.

As a consequence of greater public scrutiny following its disastrous policies in East Asia, the Fund could no longer pretend that adjustment had not been a massive failure in Africa, Latin America and South Asia. During the World Bank–IMF meetings in September 1999, the Fund conceded failure by renaming the extended structural adjustment facility (ESAF) the 'poverty reduction and growth facility' and promised to learn from the World Bank in making the elimination of poverty the 'centrepiece' of its programmes. But this was too little, too late, and too incredible. Support for the IMF in Washington was down to the US Treasury by the end of the Clinton administration.

Meltzer and the World Bank

Since assuming office in 1996, Australian-turned-American Jim Wolfensohn, by opening up channels of communication with the non-governmental organizations (NGOs) and with the help of a well-oiled public relations machine, tried to recast the Bank's image as an institution that was not only moving away from structural adjustment but was also making poverty elimination its central mission, promoting good governance, and supporting environmentally sensitive lending. The best defence, in short, was to expand the agency's agenda.

The report of the Meltzer Commission found its mark in February 2000. Exhaustively examining documents and interviewing all kinds of experts, the Commission came up with a number of devastating findings that bear being pointed out: 70 per cent of the Bank's non-grant lending is concentrated in eleven countries, with 145 other member countries left to scramble for the remaining 30 per cent; 80 per cent of the Bank's resources are devoted not to the poorest developing countries but to the better-off ones that have positive credit ratings and, according to the Commission, can therefore raise their funds in international capital markets; the failure rate of bank projects is 65–70 per cent in the poorest countries and 55–60 per cent in all developing countries. In short, the World Bank was irrelevant to the achievement of its avowed mission of global poverty alleviation.[5]

And what to do with the Bank? The Commission urged that most of the Bank's lending activities be devolved to the regional developing banks. It does not take much for readers of the report to realize that, as one of the Commission's members revealed, it 'essentially wants to abolish the International Monetary Fund and the World bank', a goal that had 'significant pockets of support … in our Congress'.[6]

Much to the chagrin of Wolfensohn, few people came to the defence of the Bank. Instead, the realities of the Bank's expanded mission were exposed in the months leading up to the World Bank–IMF meeting in Prague in September 2000.[7] The claim that the Bank was concerned about 'good governance' was contradicted by the exposure of its profound involvement with the Suharto regime in Indonesia, to which it funnelled over $30 billion in thirty years. According to several reports, including a World Bank internal report that came out in 1999, the Bank tolerated corruption, accorded false status to false government statistics, legitimized the dictatorship by passing it off as a model for other countries, and was complacent about the state of human rights and the monopolistic control of the economy. That this close embrace of the Suharto regime continued well into the Wolfensohn era was particularly damning.

The image of a new, environmentally sensitive Bank under Wolfensohn also evaporated in the avalanche of criticism that came after the Meltzer Report. The Bank was a staunch backer of the controversial Chad–Cameroon pipeline, which would seriously damage ecologically sensitive areas such as Cameroon's Atlantic Littoral Forest. Bank management was caught violating its own rules on environment and resettlement when it tried to push through the China Western Poverty Project that would have transformed an arid ecosystem supporting minority Tibetan and Mongolian sheepherders into land for settled agriculture for people from other parts of China.

A look at the bank's loan portfolio revealed the reality behind the rhetoric: loans for the environment as a percentage of the Bank's total loan portfolio declined from 3.6 per cent in fiscal year 1994 to 1.02 per cent in 1998; funds allocated to environmental projects declined by 32.7 per cent between 1998 and 1999; and more than half of all lending by the World Bank's private sector divisions in 1998 was for environmentally harmful projects like dams, roads and power. So marginalized was the Bank's environmental staff within the bureaucracy that Herman Daly, the distinguished ecological economist, left the Bank staff because he felt that he and other in-house environmentalists were having no impact at all on agency policy.

Confronted with a list of thoroughly documented charges from civil society groups during the now famous Prague Castle debate sponsored by Czech President Vaclav Havel during the tumultuous IMF–World Bank meeting on September 23, 2000, Wolfensohn was reduced to giving the memorable answer, 'I and my colleagues feel good about going to work everyday.' [8] It was an answer that underlined the depth of the Bretton Woods system crisis of legitimacy, and was matched only by IMF managing director Horst Koehler's famous line at that same event: 'I also have a heart, but I have to use my head in making decisions.'[9]

The WTO on the Road to Seattle

In the mid-1990s, the WTO was sold to the global public as the linchpin of a multilateral system of economic governance that would provide the necessary rules to facilitate the growth of global trade and the spread of its beneficial effects. Nearly five years later, the implications and consequences of the founding of the WTO had become as clear to large numbers of people as a robbery carried out in broad daylight. What were some of these realizations?

- By agreeing to eliminate import quotas and signing the Agreement on Trade Related Investment Measures (TRIMs), which declared such mechanisms as local-content policies and trade balancing requirements illegal, developing countries discovered that they had signed away their right to use trade policy as a means of industrialization.
- By signing the Agreement on Trade-Related Intellectual Property Rights (TRIPs), countries realized that they had given high-tech transnationals such as Microsoft and Intel the right to monopolize innovation in the knowledge-intensive industries, and provided biotechnology firms such as Novartis and Monsanto the go-signal to privatize the fruits of aeons of creative interaction between human communities and nature such as seeds, plants and animal life.
- By signing the Agreement on Agriculture (AOA), developing countries discovered that they had agreed to open up their markets while allowing the big agricultural superpowers to consolidate their system of subsidized agricultural production that was leading to the massive dumping of surpluses on those very markets, a process that was, in turn, destroying smallholder-based agriculture. The figures spoke for themselves: the level of overall subsidization of agriculture in the Organisation for Economic Co-operation and Development (OECD) countries rose from $182 billion in 1995 when the WTO was born, to $280 billion in 1997, to $362 billion in 1998! Instead of the beginning of a New Deal, the AOA, in the words of a former Philippine secretary of trade, 'has perpetuated the unevenness of a playing field which the multilateral trading system has been trying to correct. Moreover, this has placed the burden of

adjustment on developing countries relative to countries who can afford to maintain high levels of domestic support and export subsidies.'[10]

In contrast to the loose GATT framework, which had allowed some space for development initiatives, the comprehensive and tightened Uruguay Round was fundamentally anti-development in its thrust. This was evident in the GATT–WTO Agreement's watering down of the principle of 'Special and Differential Treatment' (SDT) for developing countries. A central pillar of UNCTAD – an organization disempowered by the establishment of the WTO – the SDT principle held that because of the critical nexus between trade and development, developing countries should not be subjected to the same expectations, rules and regulations that govern trade among the developed countries. Owing to historical and structural considerations, developing countries needed special consideration and special assistance in levelling the playing field for them to be able to participate equitably in world trade. This would include both the use of protective tariffs for development purposes and preferential access of developing country exports to developed country markets.

While GATT was not centrally concerned with development, it did recognize the 'special and differential status' of the developing countries. Perhaps the strongest statement of this was in the Tokyo Round Declaration in 1973, which recognized 'the importance of the application of differential measures in developing countries in ways which will provide special and more favorable treatment for them in areas of negotiation where this is feasible'.[11]

Different sections of the evolving GATT code allowed developing countries to renegotiate tariff bindings in order to promote the establishment of certain industries; to use tariffs for economic development and fiscal purposes; to use quantitative restrictions to promote infant industries; and conceded the principle of non-reciprocity by developing countries in trade negotiation.[12] The 1979 framework agreement known as the enabling clause also provided a permanent legal basis for general system of preferences (GSP) schemes that would provide preferential access to developing country exports.[13]

A significant shift occurred in the Uruguay Round. GSP schemes were not bound, meaning tariffs could be raised against developing countries until they equalled the bound rates applied to imports for all sources. During the negotiations, the threat to remove GSP was used as 'a form of bilateral pressure on developing countries'.[14] Special and differential treatment (SDT) was turned from a focus on a special right to protect and special rights of market access to 'one of responding to special adjustment difficulties in developing countries stemming from the implementation of WTO decisions'.[15] Measures meant to address the structural inequality of the trading system gave way to measures, such as a lower rate of tariff reduction or a longer time frame for implementing decisions, which regarded the problem of developing countries as simply that of catching up in an essentially even playing field.

SDT was significantly watered down in the WTO, and this was not surprising in view of the neoliberal agenda that underpins the WTO philosophy, which differs from the Keynesian assumptions of GATT: that there are no special rights, no special protections needed for development. The only route to development is one that involves radical trade (and investment) liberalization.

Also leading to the developing countries' disillusionment with the GATT–WTO was the fate of the measures approved during the Uruguay Round that were supposed to respond to the special conditions of developing countries. There were two key agreements, which promoters of the WTO claimed were specifically designed to meet the needs of the South: the special ministerial agreement approved in Marrakesh in April 1994, which decreed that special compensatory measures would be taken to counteract the negative effects of trade liberalization on the net food-importing developing countries; and the Agreement on Textiles and Clothing, which mandated that the system of quotas on developing country exports of textiles and garments to the North would be dismantled over ten years.

The special ministerial decision taken at Marrakesh to provide assistance to 'net food importing countries' to offset the reduction of subsidies that would make food imports more expensive for the 'net food importing countries' has never been implemented. Although world crude oil prices more than doubled in 1995–96, the World Bank and the IMF scotched any idea of offsetting aid by arguing that 'the price increase was not due to the agreement on agriculture, and besides there was never any agreement anyway on who would be responsible for providing the assistance'.[16]

The Agreement on Textiles and Clothing committed the developed countries to bring under WTO discipline all textile and garment imports over four stages, ending on January 1, 2005. A key feature was supposed to be the lifting of quotas on imports restricted under the Multi-Fibre Agreement (MFA) and similar schemes which had been used to contain penetration of developed country markets by cheap clothing and textile imports from the Third World. However, developed countries retained the right to choose which product lines to liberalize and when, so that they first brought mainly unrestricted products into the WTO discipline and postponed dealing with restricted products until much later. Thus, in the first phase, all restricted products continued to be under quota, as only items where imports were not considered threatening – such as felt hats or yarn of carded fine animal hair – were included in the developed countries' notifications. Indeed, the notifications for the coverage of products for liberalization on January 1, 1998 showed that 'even at the second stage of implementation only a very small proportion' of restricted products would see their quotas lifted.[17]

Given this trend, John Whalley notes that 'the belief is now widely held in the developing world that in 2004, while the MFA may disappear, it may well be replaced by a series of other trade instruments, possibly substantial increases in anti-dumping duties'.[18] Seattle was a cataclysm waiting to happen.

Notes

1. C. Fred Bergsten, 'The Backlash Against Globalization', speech delivered at the 2000 Meeting of the Trilateral Commission, Tokyo, April 2000 (downloaded from Internet).

2. 'Global Capitalism: Can It be Made to Work Better?', *Business Week*, November 6, 2000, pp. 42–3.

3. Ibid.

4. Quoted in Walden Bello, 'Washington's Political Transition Threatens Bretton Woods Twins', in Walden Bello, *The Future in the Balance* (Oakland, CA: Food First, 2001), p. 238.

5. International Financial Institutions Advisory Commission, *Report* (Washington, DC: US Congress, 2000).

6. C. Fred Bergsten, 'The Backlash … '.

7. The following facts and statistics were drawn from various sources and brought together in Walden Bello, 'Hard Answers Please, Mr. Wolfensohn and Mr. Kohler', speech delivered at the Prague Castle Debate, Prague, September 23, 2000.

8. Statement at the Prague Castle Debate, September 23, 2000.

9. Ibid.

10. Cesar Bautista, speech at the Second Ministerial of the World Trade Organization, Geneva, May 18–20, 1998.

11. Quoted in John Whalley, 'Special and Differential Treatment in the Millennium Round', *CSGR Working Paper*, No. 30/99 (May 1999), p. 3.

12. Ibid., p. 4.

13. Ibid., p. 7.

14. Ibid., p. 10.

15. Ibid., p. 14.

16. 'More Power to the World Trade Organization', *Panos Briefing*, November 1999, p. 14.

17. South Center, *The Multilateral Trade Agenda and the South* (Geneva: South Center, 1998), p. 32.

18. John Whalley, 'Building Poor Countries' Trading Capacity', *CSGR Working Paper Series* (Warwick: CSGR, March 1999).

FIVE
The Vicissitudes of Reform, 1998–2002

With the onset of the Asian financial crisis, the role of the G7 in co-ordinating the response to the need change in the institutions of global economic governance became especially acute. This was particularly clear in relation to the Asian financial crisis.

Reforming the Global Financial Architecture

Calls for a new global financial architecture to reduce the volatility of the trillions of dollars shooting around the world in pursuit of narrow but significant interest rate differentials came from many quarters in the wake of the crisis. Eventually, the USA evolved the position that the current architecture was basically sound, there was no need for major reforms, and what was needed was simply 'improving the wiring of the system'. Though there were some differences on some details, this position was shared by the other members of the G-7.

This approach assigned primacy to 'reforming' the financial sectors of the crisis economies through increased transparency, tougher bankruptcy laws to eliminate moral hazard, prudential regulation using the 'core principles' drafted by the Basle committee on banking supervision, and greater inflow of foreign capital not only to recapitalize shattered banks, but also to 'stabilize' the local financial system by making foreign interests integral to it.

When it came to the supply-side actors in the North, this

perspective would leave them to comply voluntarily with the Basle principles. Although government intervention might be needed periodically to catch free-falling casino players whose collapse might bring down the whole global financial structure (as was the case in late 1998 when a consortium of New York banks – led by the Reserve Bank of New York – organized a rescue of the hedge fund Long-Term Capital Management after the latter was unravelled by Russia's financial crisis). The furthest the G-7 has gone in terms of dealing with the controversial hedge fund question was to issue a declaration in October 1998 commenting on the need to examine 'the implications arising from the operations of leveraged international financial organizations including hedge funds and offshore institutions' and 'to encourage offshore centers to comply with internationally agreed standards'.[1]

Tobin taxes or similar controls designed to slow down capital flows were a no-no. Instead even more liberalization was seen as the answer to global financial instability. US Treasury Secretary Larry Summers revealed the logic behind this approach in his comments on Argentina in 1999: 'Today, fully 50 per cent of the banking sector, 70 per cent of private banks, in Argentina are foreign-controlled, up from 30 per cent in 1994. The result is a deeper, more efficient market, and external investors with a greater stake in staying put.'[2] To put it in the curious algebra of the US Treasury, financial liberalization equals domestic financial stability equals the global interest.

When it came to IMF reform, no substantial reforms were offered in the area of policy. To all intents and purposes an unreformed IMF continued to be at the centre of the 'firefighting system'. Indeed, the G-7 supported the expansion of the powers of the IMF. On the one hand, it gave the Fund the authority to push private creditors to carry some of the costs of a rescue programme, that is, to 'bail them in' instead of bailing them out. This was a modest response to clamour on both the right and the left that because the Fund had been used in the past to bail out private creditors, they were merely encouraged to engage in more irresponsible lending in the future.

On the other hand, the G-7 authorized the creation of a 'contingency credit line' that would be made available to countries that are about to be subjected to speculative attack. Access to these funds would be dependent on a country's track record in terms of observing good macroeconomic fundamentals, as traditionally stipulated by the Fund.

The only problem with the latter proposal was that no one wanted to avail themselves of the pre-crisis credit line, rightly worried that speculative investors would take this as a sign of crisis and move to take their capital out of the country, thus accelerating the crisis that the pre-crisis credit line was supposed to avert in the first place.

Another innovation that was trumpeted by the G-7 in the area of global financial management was the creation of a 'Financial Stability Forum'. As originally proposed, this body had no representation from the less developed economies. When this generated criticism, the G-7 issued an invitation to Singapore and Hong Kong to join the body. The developing countries were still not satisfied, however, leading the G-7 to create the G-20, with more representation from the South. As Andy Knight notes, however, even this expanded G-20 has no representation from the poorest developing countries.[3] Moreover, 'The G-20 also lacks any mechanism for reporting or for accountability to the broader international community; its origins in the G-7 reduce its legitimacy; its membership is not fully representative; its mandate is narrow; its procedures are not inclusive enough to allow for participation by non-governmental organizations; and, its operations are not all that transparent either.'[4]

But probably the biggest indicator of the bankruptcy of the G-7 in the area of financial architecture reform has been its inability to come up with a viable mechanism to deal with cases of national bankruptcy. Ever since the Third World debt crisis in the early 1980s, suggestions would be made periodically that an international bankruptcy mechanism needed to be established, something that would be the equivalent of the US Chapter 11 at the international level, where the entities that could file for bankruptcy and reorganization would not be countries. The Asian financial crisis and the subsequent crises in Russia and Brazil in 1998 revived interest in such a mechanism. It was, however, the collapse of the Argentine economy in the first quarter of 2002 under a heavy debt load that underlined the urgency of establishing one.

When, on April 1, 2002, Ann Krueger, the American citizen who is currently deputy director of the IMF, voiced her support for 'a single international judicial entity' to oversee and arbitrate debt restructuring, the idea seemed to have finally gained momentum. The very next day, however, John Taylor, the international undersecretary of the US Treasury, disagreed, saying that the 'most practical and broadly acceptable reform would be to have sovereign borrowers and their creditors put a package of new clauses in the debt contracts'.[5] In other words, specify some conditions for repayment in the event of a debt crisis, but let the matter remain a concern between the sovereign borrower and its creditors – in short, the status quo, where the creditors tend to unite and have tremendous advantage over the debtor.[6] In the face of opposition from her own government, Krueger retreated, and Argentina was left to twist in the wind – though any relief an IMF-connected bankruptcy court might have offered would probably have been scant in the first place.

From Structural Adjustment to Poverty Reduction?

With the disaster of structural adjustment becoming more evident in developing countries, the G-7 committed itself to achieve, with the leadership of the World Bank, a significant reduction in the debt servicing of the forty-one highly indebted poor countries (HIPC). This commitment was most loudly proclaimed at the G-7 meeting in Cologne in July 1999. Yet at the Okinawa Summit the following year, debt reduction for the poor countries did not figure in the agenda, and during the Genoa Summit in July 2001, it received only perfunctory mention in the final communiqué. This was not surprising because the actual debt reduction achieved by the programme since it began in 1996 was only $1 billion – or a reduction of their debt servicing by only 3 per cent in four and a half years.[7] Another estimate, by the British NGO Christian Aid, is that only 6.4 per cent of the total debt of the world's poorest countries would be tackled by the HIPC initiative.[8] And the World Bank itself admitted that the half of the countries covered by HIPC programme would still have unsustainable debt loads at the end of their programme.[9] According to the Jubilee USA analysis, the programme was failing, miserably, because it was too long, there was too little debt relief, countries were forced to commit to unreasonable conditions, and countries' debt relief was tied to their living up to restrictive IMF conditionalities.[10]

At the World Bank–IMF meeting in the autumn of 1999, the extended structural adjustment facility (ESAF) was renamed the poverty reduction and growth facility. Along with this change was supposed to come a basic change in approach. As US Treasury Secretary Larry Summers put it, the new approach would consist of 'moving away from an IMF-centered process that has too often focused on narrow macroeconomic objectives at the expense of broader human development'.[8] The new process would be 'a new more inclusive process that would involve multiple international organizations and give national policy makers and civil society groups a more central role'.[9]

But the new approach, on closer inspection, was suspiciously like the old one. Summers stated that the new IMF must have as one of its priorities 'strong support for market opening and trade liberalization'.[10] Trade liberalization, he continued,

> is often a key component of IMF arrangements. In the course of negotiations, the IMF has sought continued compliance with existing trade obligations and further commitments to market

opening measures as part of a strategy of spurring growth. For example: As part of its IMF program, Indonesia has abolished import monopolies for soybeans and wheat; agreed to phase out all non-tariff barriers affecting imports; dissolved all cartels for plywood, cement, and paper; removed restrictions on foreign investments in the wholesale and resale trades; and allowed foreign banks to buy domestic ones. Zambia's 1999 program with the IMF commits the government to reducing the weighted average tariff on foreign goods to ten per cent, and to cutting the maximum tariff from 25 to 20 per cent in 2001. In July, the import ban on wheat flour was eliminated.[11]

In other words, beneath the rhetoric of anti-poverty and human development, the same neoliberal economic model prevailed.

As for the PRSP process – the preparation of poverty reduction strategy papers between Fund, Bank and local government officials – this turned out to be nothing more than an effort to add a veneer of public participation and anti-poverty rhetoric to the same technocratic process and model emphasizing liberalization and deregulation. Recent reports coming in from countries where the PRSP process has begun

> show that little has changed in the IMF–World Bank's approach to programming either in content or in process. Experiences from Bolivia, Nicaragua, Tanzania, Zambia, and Mozambique indicate that PRSP processes continue to be based on existing structural adjustment frameworks and macroeconomic indicators, with little more than lip service to genuine public participation in poverty analyses and policy formulation.[12]

Moreover, participation has involved

> little more than consultations with a few prominent and liberal CSO's, rather than broad-based, substantive public dialogue about the causes of incidence of poverty. Local, vernacular forms of civil society organization such as labour unions, peasant organizations, social movements, women's groups, and indigenous people's

organizations have not been invited into the process, and the little public discussion that has taken place has been limited to well resourced national and international non-governmental organizations.[13]

A detailed look at the PRSPs for three countries – Vietnam, Laos and Cambodia – by Focus on the Global South analysts Joy Chavez Malaluan and Shalmali Guttal reinforces the above observations. Beneath the thick rhetoric of poverty alleviation, the so-called consultative process reveals the same one-size-fits-all policy matrix emphasizing rapid growth, the deregulation of monetary policy, the tearing down of the state sector in favour of private enterprises, deregulation, more liberal foreign investment laws, trade liberalization, export-oriented growth and commercialization of land and resource rights.

'The PRSP is upheld by the World Bank and the IMF as a comprehensive approach,' note the authors. 'That it certainly is,' they conclude, 'but not for poverty reduction. The PRSP is a comprehensive program for structural adjustment, in the name of the poor.'[14]

The more things change, the more they remain the same – this aphorism has been never more true than in the case of the World Bank. That the drive for reform at the Bank had been stymied was revealed dramatically by the easing out of two highly regarded economists: Joseph Stiglitz, the chief economist (owing to pressure from US Treasury Secretary Larry Summers, his orthodox predecessor) and Ravi Kanbur, head of the World Development Task Force (owing to pressure from the Bank's entrenched policy analysts).

Non-democratic decision-making affirmed

When it comes to the issue of democratizing the IMF and the World Bank, there is no longer any talk about doing away with the feudal practices of always having an American head the Bank and a European to lead the Fund. In terms of giving more voting power to developing countries, many proposals have been made over the last three years. Perhaps the most prominent of these has been associated with Joseph Stiglitz, the former chief economist. Stiglitz's not unreasonable proposal is that 'pending a reexamination of the allocation of voting, the direct voice of the borrowing countries in the executive boards of the IFI's be increased, e.g., by establishing two additional seats with half votes, or repackaging constituencies'.[15]

Such proposals have not even reached first base, and the reason is, as Mark Zacher notes, that

> it is very unlikely that the major donor states (namely, the Western industrialized countries) are going to sacrifice their veto power (15, 30, and 50 per cent of total votes depending on the issue) over the amount of money that they contribute or the policies concerning loans and grants to recipient countries. They may be willing to make some modest changes in the distribution of votes and the majorities that are required for particular types of decisions; but they are not going to sacrifice their ability to block decisions that concern contributions to the IMF and the IMF's dispersements [sic] of these funds.[16]

Decision-making at the WTO: from Seattle to Doha

As for the World Trade Organization, instead of seeking to change the blatantly unrepresentative decision-making processes after the Seattle fiasco, WTO officials have been busy defending them. The Green Room process was, for instance, defended thus by a key adviser to Director-General Mike Moore: 'One of the myths about Seattle is that there were no Africans and hardly any developing countries in the Green Room. In fact, there were six Africans and a majority from developing countries. Moreover, any deal reached in the Green Room must still be approved by all WTO members.'[17] Mike Moore himself told developing country delegates at the UNCTAD X meeting in Bangkok in February 2000 that the Consensus/Green Room system was 'non-negotiable'.[18]

The lack of movement towards a more transparent and democratic decision-making process was more than evident in the lead-up to and in the proceedings of the Fourth Ministerial in Doha, Qatar, in November 2001.

The proposed draft declaration for the Ministerial meeting was a product of the sort of non-transparent tactics to which the big trading powers resorted. In the lead-up to Doha, most of the developing countries were pretty much united around the position that the Ministerial would have to focus on implementation issues and on reviews of key WTO agreements, not on launching a new round of trade liberalization.

But when the draft declaration came out a few weeks before Doha, the emphasis was not on dealing with implementation issues, but on an alleged consensus on opening up negotiations on the issues of competition, investment policy, government procurement and trade facilitation that were the priorities of the minority of rich and powerful trading countries. 'Despite clearly stated positions that the developing countries are unwilling to go into a new round until past implementation and decision-making are addressed,' noted Aileen Kwa, who followed the process closely, 'the draft declaration favorably positioned the launching of a comprehensive new round with an open agenda.'[19]

The draft, authored by the chair of the General Council, was a product of consultations with all WTO members. In actual fact, the key consultations were conducted among an inner circle of between twenty and twenty-five participants – the so-called Green Room process, which effectively excludes most of the members of the WTO. In the lead-up to Qatar, this exclusive process held two 'mini-Ministerials', one in Mexico at the end of August and another in Singapore on October 13–14. How one got invited to these meetings was very murky. Aileen Kwa cites the case of one ambassador from a transition economy who was promised an invitation to a Green Room meeting by the WTO Secretariat but never got one. Then there was the case of an African ambassador who wanted to attend the Singapore mini-Ministerial: when he approached the WTO secretariat for an invitation, he was told that they were not hosting the meeting. When he tried the Singapore mission in Geneva, the response was that they were simply co-ordinating the meeting and were not in a position to send out invitations.[20]

The Doha Ministerial from November 9 to 14, 2001, took place amid conditions that were already unfavourable from the point of view of developing country interests. The September 11 events provided a heaven-sent opportunity for US Trade Representative Robert Zoellick and European Union Trade Commissioner Pascal Lamy to step up the pressure on the developing countries to agree to the launching of a new trade round, invoking the rationale that it was necessary to counter a global downturn that had been worsened by the terrorist actions. The location was also unfavourable, Qatar being a monarchy where dissent could be easily controlled. The WTO Secretariat's authority over who would be granted visas to enter Qatar for the Ministerial allowed it radically to limit the number of legitimate NGOs that could be present to about sixty, thus preventing that explosive interaction of developing country resentment and massive street protest that took place in Seattle.

Still, these factors would not have been sufficient to bring about an unfavourable outcome. Tactics mattered, and here the developing countries were clearly outmanoeuvred in Doha. Among these tactics the following must be highlighted:[21]

• Pushing the highly unbalanced draft declaration and presenting it to the Ministerial as a 'clean text' on which there allegedly was consensus, thus restricting the arena of substantive discussion and making it difficult for developing countries to register fundamental objections without seeming 'obstructionist'.

- Pitting officials from the capitals against their negotiators based in Geneva, with the latter being characterized as 'recalcitrant' or 'narrow'.
- Employing direct threats, as the United States did when it warned Haiti and the Dominican Republic to cease opposition to its position on government procurement or risk cancellation of their preferential trade arrangements.
- Buying off countries with goodies, as the European Union did when, in return for their agreeing to the final declaration, it assured countries in the ACP (Africa-Caribbean-Pacific) group that the WTO would respect the so-called 'ACP Waiver' that would allow them to export their agricultural commodities to Europe at preferential terms relative to other developing countries. Pakistan, a stalwart among developing countries in Geneva, was notably quiet at Doha. Apparently, this had something to do with the USA's granting Pakistan a massive aid package of grants, loans and debt reduction owing to its special status in the US war against terrorism. Nigeria had taken the step of issuing an official communiqué denouncing the draft declaration before Doha, but came out loudly supporting it on November 14 – a flip-flop that is difficult to separate from the USA's coming up with the promise of a big economic and military aid package in the interim.
- Reinstituting the infamous 'Green Room' on November 13 and 14, when some twenty hand-picked countries were isolated from the rest and 'delegated' by the WTO secretariat and the big powers to come up with the final declaration. These countries were not picked by a democratic process, and efforts by some developing country representatives to insert themselves into this select group were rebuffed, some gently, others quite explicitly, as was the case with a delegate from Uganda.
- Finally, pressuring the developing countries by telling them that they would bear the onus for causing the collapse of another Ministerial, the collapse of the WTO and the

deepening of the global recession that would allegedly be the consequence of these two events.

Doha was a low point in the GATT–WTO's history of backroom intimidation, threats, bribery and non-transparency. There are no records of the actual decision-making process in Doha because the formal sessions of the Ministerial – which is where decision-making is made in a democratic system – were, as in Seattle, reserved for speeches, and the real decisions took place in informal groupings whose meeting places kept shifting and were not known to all. There being no records, there is little accountability and the principals in any deals can deny that they engaged in questionable behaviour.

This non-transparent process resulted in practically sidelining the developing countries' demand that the WTO focus on implementation issues and placing on centre stage the top agenda of the big trading powers: the eventual launching of a new set of trade negotiations that would bring under WTO jurisdiction the non-trade areas of investment, competition policy, government procurement and trade facilitation. C. Fred Bergsten, the free-trade partisan, once compared the WTO and trade liberalization to a bicycle: it stays upright only by moving forward. Doha set the WTO upright once more, but it is still wobbly, and this is because a great deal of resentment lingers among developing countries from the whole non-transparent process of bamboozling them into accepting a declaration running counter to their interests. The WTO's crisis of legitimacy is not over, and the non-transparency and lack of democracy so evident in Doha may yet deepen it.

Notes

1. Quoted in United Nations, *Toward a New Financial Architecture: A Report of the Task Force of the Executive Committee on Economic and Social Affairs of the United Nations* (New York: UNCTAD, 1999).

2. Quoted in Walden Bello, 'Power, Timidity, and Irresponsibility in Global Finance', in *The Future in the Balance*, p. 159.

3. W. Andy Knight, 'Multilevel Economic Governance through Subsidiarity: Remodelling the Global Financial Architecture', paper prepared for the Conference on the International Financial Architecture, Center for Global Studies, University of Victoria, August 29–30, 2001.

4. Ibid.

5. Quoted in Nicola Bullard, 'The Puppet Master Shows His Hand', *Focus on Trade*, No. 76, April 2002, pp. 3–4.

6. Ibid.

7. These estimates come from Eric Toussaint of CADTIM.

8. Cited in 'HIPC: The Official Debt Relief Program', Jubilee 2000/USA Fact Sheet, June 2002.

9. Cited in Soren Ambrose and Mara Vanderslice, 'G7 Debt Relief Plan: More Grief than Relief', Spotlight, Jubilee US Network, June 2002.

10. Ibid.

11. Op-ed piece in *Washington Post*, reproduced in *Today*, November 15, 1999.

12. Ibid.

13. US Treasury Secretary Larry Summers, testimony before the US Senate Committee on Foreign Relations, Washington, DC, November 5, 1999.

14. Ibid.

15. Shalmali Guttal, 'The End of Imagination: The World Bank, the International Monetary Fund, and Poverty Reduction', Bangkok, Focus on the Global South, September 2000.

16. Ibid.

17. Jenina Joy Chavez Malaluan and Shalmali Guttal, 'Structural Adjustment in the Name of the Poor: The PRSP Experience in the Lao PDR, Cambodia, and Vietnam', Bangkok, Focus on the Global South, January 2002, p. 18.

18. Proposal presented at the Conference on International Financial Architecture, University of British Columbia at Victoria, August 29–30, 2001.

19. Mark Zacher, ibid.

20. Philip Legrain, 'Should the WTO be Aboloished?', *Ecologist*, Vol. 30, No. 9, December 2000/January 1, 2001, p. 23.

21. Statement at UNCTAD X, Bangkok, February 2000.

22. Aileen Kwa, 'Crisis in WTO Talks', *Focus on Trade*, No. 68, October 2001.

23. Ibid.

24. The following account is based on discussions among participants, many of whom attended the Doha Ministerial, at the consultation held in Brussels of the 'Our World is not for Sale Coalition' on December 9–11, 2002.

SIX

Proposals for Global Governance Reform: A Critical Analysis

An Economic Security Council?

Aside from reform proposals for the WTO and Bretton Woods institutions, among the key ideas advanced in the last few years has been the creation of an Economic Security Council (ESC), a suggestion associated with the Commission on Global Governance. According to the Commission, the ESC would have the same status in the UN hierarchy as the Security Council but be independent of it.

The ESC would be a sort of international economic directorate – an 'apex body' that would serve as the 'focal point for global economic governance'. A key function of this body

> would be to bridge the gap between the various international economic insitutions. This does not mean there has to be centrally coordinated direction of all the world's institutions of economic governance under one umbrella. That would be neither feasible not desirable. What is required is agreement on goals, roles, and mandates ...
>
> At a practical level, the ESC and its staff would expect to work closely with staff from the Bretton Woods institutions and the GATT/WTO, breaking down the institutional isolation that currently exists, as well as with bodies such as the International Labour Organization (ILO), to underline the social dimensions of its functions.[1]

Establishment of the ESC would be accompanied by a 'rational-

ization' of Bretton Woods and UN institutions, with the Commission recommending closing down UNCTAD and UNIDO and
suggesting that were it to come into being, 'governments may
want to consider whether it is necessary to continue the work of
the Development and Interim Committees'.[2]

Ever since it was floated in 1995, the ESC has not gained
much support from either developed or developing countries. A
new superbody with significant developing country membership
to which the Bretton Woods institutions and the WTO would
'report' was not bound to excite the developed countries. At the
same time, the proposal that 'the world's largest economies would
be represented as of right', while others would not be in a twenty-
three-member body did not appeal to the developing countries.

Moreover, developing countries were not happy with the
recommendation to abolish UNCTAD and move its functions
to the WTO,[3] since UNCTAD had been, after all, one of the few
agencies in the UN system that had consistently championed the
interests of the Third World. Equally important was the sense that
because of inevitable dominance by the developed countries, the
ESC superbody would simply translate into a centralization of
rich country control over the global economy, especially since
the ESC would need to work close with the rich-country-
dominated WTO and Bretton Woods institutions.

The Meltzer Commission Proposal

As noted earlier, the report of the International Financial Institution Advisory Commission, better known as the 'Meltzer Report'
after its chairman Alan Meltzer, launched a devastating attack on
the performance of the World Bank and the IMF that served as
a striking confirmation from the mainstream of what a whole
generation of progressive critics had been saying for the last
twenty-five years.[4] Among the most important conclusions of
the report were the following:

- instead of promoting economic growth, the IMF institution-alizes economic stagnation;
- the World Bank is irrelevant rather than central to the goal of eliminating global poverty;
- both institutions are to a great extent driven by the interests of key political and economic institutions in the G-7 countries – particularly, the US government and US financial interests;
- the dynamics of both institutions derive not so much from the external demands of poverty alleviation or promoting growth as from the internal imperative of bureaucratic empire-building.

While diplomatic in its language when discussing the IMF, the report finds little of value in the institution. It shows that the Fund's foray into macroeconomic reform via structural adjustment institutionalized economic stagnation, poverty and inequality in Africa and Latin America is the 1980s and 1990s.

It confirms that the Fund's original objective of ensuring a stable global financial order was derailed by its prescription of indiscriminate capital account liberalization for the countries of East Asia, its habit of assembling financial rescue packages that simply encouraged 'moral hazard' of irresponsible lending and speculative investment, and its prescribing tight fiscal and monet-ary policies that merely worsened the situation in the countries hit by the Asian financial crisis instead of reversing it.

The report recommends shutting down Fund programmes such as the extended structural adjustment programme, now renamed the 'Poverty Reduction Strategy Program', and downsizing the IMF. Inexplicably, however, in view of its unsparing criticism, it recommends that the IMF should continue in and consolidate its role of being a 'quasi-lender of last resort' to countries suffering a liquidity crisis. By the Commission's own account, this is a task that the Fund has handled badly in the past. Moreover, the Com-mission's recommending of strict conditions under which it may extend credit contradicts its own criticism of 'the use of IMF resources and conditionality to control the economies of developing nations'.[5]

Particularly objectionable is the Commission's proposal that the Fund provide liquidity assistance only to those countries that 'permit freedom of entry and operation to foreign financial institutions' on the grounds that these entities would, among other things, 'stabilize and develop the local financial system'. This is problematic for two reasons. First, foreign financial institutions such as hedge funds, which have taken full advantage of 'free entry and operation', have helped precipitate one financial crisis after another. Second, forcing countries to adopt Western-style free market norms governing the ownership of foreign financial subsidiaries and their local operations violates the first core principle that the Commission endorses for IMF reform – that is, 'the desire to ensure that democratic processes and sovereign authority are respected in both borrowing and lending countries'.[6]

This contradiction between the logic of the analysis and the prescription is a reminder that the Commission was, after all, a US government-appointed body, many of whose members came from the banking sector, conservative think-tanks and establishment universities who are very wary about placing significant restrictions on the free flow of finance capital globally, even when the evidence they are staring at underlines the destructiveness of unchecked capital mobility.

When it deals with the World Bank, the Commission draws a picture of a massive institution that is driven to lend more by instititutional imperatives than actual need in the recipient countries, that is burdened by high failure rates both in its project lending and its programme (structural adjustment) lending, that has poor monitoring capabilities of the sustainability of its projects, that competes rather than supplements the regional development banks.

The Commission proposes the transformation of the World Bank into a World Development Authority that would give only grant aid and technical assistance. It would also have the Bank devolve its loan programmes to the regional development banks.

To take the second proposal first, evolution and decentralization are fine principles, but they are no solution if the regional institution has the same structure, operating style and paradigm of development as the World Bank. This is certainly the case with the Asian Development Bank, which has had the same record of high project failure rates, the same lack of accountability and the same macroeconomic approach as the World Bank.[7] The other components of the multilateral aid system must, in short, also be restructured, since they are satellites orbiting around the World Bank.

As for the proposal to turn the Bank into a centralized concessional aid agency, this is no solution at all since the problem lies not in the function of the Bank but in its structure, approach and ideology. It is hard not to imagine it bringing to the management of concessional aid the same problems it has had in the administration of loans. Moreover, the World Development Authority would not eliminate the power imbalance that is one of the key problems with the World Bank and the Bretton Woods system: control by the rich countries of the decision-making and management of aid.

The Meltzer Commission proposals, while flawed, are not to be underestimated, for they carry weight with the Bush II administrator, particularly with the influential Treasury Secretary Paulo O'Neill.

The 'Back-to-the-Bretton-Woods-System' School

The Meltzer Commission Report comes from the right of the neoclassical orthodoxy. Coming from the left or, more appropriately, centre-left are the proposals made by a number of economists and policy analysts that, for lack of a better name, we might call the 'Back-to-the-Bretton-Woods-System' School.

A key reform advanced by this school in the area of international finance would be placing tougher controls on capital flows at the global level, in the form of the Tobin tax or variants of it.[8] The Tobin tax is a transactions tax on capital inflows and outflows at all key points of the world economy that would 'throw sand in the wheels of global capital movements'. Controls at the international level may be supplemented by national level controls on capital inflows or outflows. A model of such a measure was the Chilean measure that required portfolio investors to deposit up to 30 per cent of their investment in an interest-free account at the Central Bank for a year, which was said to be succesful in discouraging massive portfolio investment inflows.[9] Among some writers, there is an ill-concealed admiration for Malaysian Prime Minister Mohamad Mahathir's tough set of measures restricting capital outflows, which were imposed in 1998. Among these measures were the fixing of the exchange rate, the withdrawal of the local currency from international circulation, and a one-year lock-in period for capital already in the country.[10]

In addition to controls at the national and international levels, proponents of this view also see regional controls as desirable and feasible. The Asian Monetary Fund (AMF) is regarded as an attractive, workable proposal that must be revived. The AMF was proposed by Japan at the height of the Asian financial crisis to serve as a pool for the foreign exchange reserves of the reserve-rich Asian countries that would repel speculative attacks on Asian currencies. Not surprisingly, Washington vetoed it.

The thrust of these international, national and regional controls is partly to prevent destabilizing waves of capital entry and exit and partly to move investment inflow from short-term portfolio investment and short-term loans to long-term direct investment and long-term loans. For some, capital controls are not simply stabilizing measures but are strategic tools, like tariffs and quotas, that may justifiably be employed to influence a country's degree and mode of integration into the global economy. In other words, capital and trade controls are legitimate instruments of trade and industrial policy aimed at national industrial development.

When it comes to the World Bank, IMF and WTO, the thrust

of this school is to reform these institutions along the lines of greater accountability, greater transparency, a greater role in decision-making by developing country governments, and less doctrinal push for free trade and capital account liberalization. Unlike the G-7, advocates of this perspective see the function of the Fund not as that of serving principally as a disciplinary tool for overspending governments but as that of infusing greater liquidity into economies in crisis, without the restrictive conditions that now accompany the lending activities of the IMF. Some analysts recommend the establishment of a World Financial Authority (WFA). The WFA's main task, in one formulation, would be to develop and impose regulations on global capital flows and serve as 'a forum within which the rules of international financial cooperation are developed and implemented ... by effective coordination of the activities of national monetary authorities'.[11]

Also suggested is the establishment of a 'Global Bankruptcy System ... which would oversee and implement bankruptcies with cross boundary claims' that would 'approach bankruptcy with a balanced perspective of the interests of creditors and borrowers, with the recognition that ... special procedures need to be devised when there are systemic bankruptcies, where the macroeconomic costs of delay in reorganization can be quite large'.[12] Unlike the proposal of IMF Deputy Director Ann Krueger, however, this mechanism would be outside the IMF.

While there are new institutions proposed, this school nevertheless still sees the Fund, World Bank and WTO continue as central institutions of a world regulatory regime. Despite his searing critique of the IMF, Stiglitz, for instance, writes that 'rather than creating new institutions, it would be better to strengthen existing international institutions'.[13] They must, however, be made more accountable and transparent and they must be prevented from imposing one common model of trade and investment on all countries. Instead of imprisoning countries in a one-shoe-fits-all model, they must provide a framework for more discriminate global integration, that would allow greater trade and investment flows but also allow some space for national differences in the organization of global capitalism.

One vision of a reformed system of multilateral governance is sketched out by Ann Florini, senior analyst at the Carnegie Endowment for International Peace. Imagining herself looking back from her vantage point in the year 2020, she sketches out what would be for her a desirable outcome:

> The two-decade experiment with ever-more-intrusive conditionality attached to loans from the international financial institutions has been widely acknowledged a failure, since the conditions generated great bitterness and did little good. The World Bank now makes few loans, giving most of its help in the form of grants and technical assistance. The IMF still serves as lender of last resort for the international system, but its conditions are now broad outcome requirements (e.g., holding international reserves above a certain level) without prescribing how countries should achieve those outcomes. Parts of the negotiations between the IMF and country officials are still often confidential, but they are no longer entirely secret talks between IMF staff and finance ministry officials. The WTO dispute resolution mechanism has evolved substantially to incorporate a much wider range of perspectives on whether a given measure is truly a protectionist barrier or a legitimate measure serving a non-trade-related end. The push to do away with all national regulations that might impede trade or foreign investment has given way to a more balanced assessment that allows equal standing to other goals.[14]

As formulated by Dani Rodrik, an influential professor of political economy at Harvard, the ideal multilateral system appears to be a throwback to the original Bretton Woods system devised by Keynes that reigned from 1945 to the mid-1970s, where 'rules left enough space for national development efforts to proceed along successful but divergent paths'.[15] In other words, a 'regime of peaceful coexistence among national capitalisms'.[16]

Not surprisingly, this 'global Keynesian' perspective has resonated well with economists and technocrats from developing countries, the devastated Asian economies and the UN system, which is well known as a refuge for Keynesians who fled the neoliberal counter-revolution at the World Bank and universities.

Some of the institutional innovations proposed by this school, such as a multi-tiered system of local, national and regional capital controls are definitely worth considering. Moreover, its advocacy for greater global space for the unfolding of distinct national strategies for development is certainly a step in the right direction. However, the Back-to-the-Bretton-Woods-System School fails satisfactorily to address the central questions. Can the World Bank, WTO and IMF really be transformed so as to allow such diversity to flourish? Are these institutions still the appropriate institutions of a system of global economic governance for an international economy built on different principles from those that now serve as their main ideological pillars? And granted that the pre-1980 global system had more space for different paths to development than the post-1980 system, do we really want to return to it?

George Soros's Alternative System

Some of the proposals of the Back-to-the-Bretton-Woods-System School people are echoed by George Soros, the financier, who has recently achieved renown for his critique of the global financial system, especially for his merciless analysis of the paradigm of 'market fundamentalism' that undergirds it. His most recent book, *On Globalization*, is a thoughtful critique of the current system of global economic governance and presents an ambitious comprehensive blueprint for reform of the WTO, the IMF and the international aid system.

Perhaps Soros stands most firmly when he deals with the WTO. Unlike many other proponents of global governance reform such as the International Confederation of Free Trade Unions (ICFTU), Soros does not propose attaching amendments such as labour or social clauses to the WTO charter. This is not, however, for the reasons given by many WTO critics, who say that this would simply give more power to an already extremely powerful organization, since the WTO would be given the mandate to be the ultimate judge in trade and labour issues. Soros supports the WTO mission of promoting 'rules-based liberalization of international trade' and believes that the WTO 'accomplishes that mission brilliantly'.[17] Soros's reason is that this would overload the WTO with a task that it is not equipped to do while hampering it in fulfilling its main role of global trade liberalization. Other institutions should either be strengthened or created to promote what Soros calls 'global public goods' such as labour rights, the environment, consumer safety and public health. The International Labour Organization (ILO), for instance, must be strengthened *vis-à-vis* the WTO, and the place to start is by forcing governments to ratify ILO conventions. Civil society, he argues, should be pressuring the US government, for instance, which has ratified only thirteen of 182 ILO conventions and only two of eight 'core labor standards'.[18]

This promising approach of urging the creation of, or strengthening, countervailing institutions devoted to public goods is nevertheless undermined by his failure to follow through on the political consequences of his analysis. Inexplicably, he does not propose coercive power for such countervailing institutions, but would limit them to eliciting 'voluntary compliance'.[19] In fact, the problem lies not in the lack of countervailing institutions – there are scores of multilateral environmental agreements and organizations; it lies in their lack of coercive power. In contrast, the WTO enjoys formal coercive power while the IMF and World Bank possess informal coercive power owing to their control over massive financial resources.

When it comes to the World Bank, Soros's reform proposals are on even more tenuous grounds. He argues that the proposal of the Meltzer Commission to convert the World Bank into a World Development Authority specializing in grants to the poorest countries is not acceptable because 'so-called middle income countries like Brazil, and even Chile, have very uneven income distributions and great social needs'.[20] He also argues for giving James Wolfensohn a chance to implement reforms such as the Comprehensive Development Framework ('CDF') or the 'Poverty Reduction Strategy Papers'. Lending operations must be reformed, there should be more consultations with civil society, loans to repressive and corrupt regimes should be stopped, directors should be made more independent of the governments they represent, and steps must be taken to prevent the staff from dominating the agency such as putting a limit of five years on employment.

The problem here is that many of these reforms have been tossed about for thirty years, ever since the tenure of Robert McNamara, yet things have not improved. As Soros himself has admitted on other occasions, the Bank's performance has simply got worse and the bureaucracy has become more immovable.[21] As noted earlier, the CDF framework and the PRSP have not meant a break with the old macroeconomic paradigm guiding both World Bank and IMF structural adjustment programmes, which stressed narrowly defined economic efficiency, greater market orientation and fiscal and monetary stability. Consultations with civil society groups have, in fact, taken place under Wolfensohn, but this has amounted to no more than a public relations exercise, the main legacy of which has been greater suspicion of the Bank by many grassroots NGOs that felt the Bank was isolating them as 'unreasonable' NGOs and dealing only with 'reasonable' ones.

As for giving Wolfensohn a chance, this is a highly personal calculus which is not likely to sound credible to pro-reform elements who have been waiting for nearly a decade since Wolfensohn's appointment as World Bank head for some improvements to take place. Critics point out that the Wolfensohn regime is in many ways a replay of the era of Robert McNamara, with the same 'anti-poverty' rhetoric and strategy, and with the same meagre results in terms of effective aid programmes.

In the end, Soros admits that keeping the World Bank afloat is only a temporary measure designed to ward off the attack of the right on multilateral aid, thus buying time to put a better aid mechanism in place.[22] That mechanism would be the issuance of special drawing rights (SDRs) via the IMF and the rich countries' donation of their share to a development fund. This would mean treating the SDR not just as a reserve currency but as a real asset to be used for development purposes. Should the rich countries agree to treat SDRs as real assets and to donate their share of the new SDRs created to aid, Soros says, there would immediately be available some $18 billion under a special SDR issue already approved by the IMF but awaiting ratification by the US Congress.

Under the proposal, an 'international board operating under the aegis of the IMF but independent of it' would be set up to decide which projects or programmes would be eligible for funding. The board would actually have no authority over the spending of funds but 'would merely prepare a menu from which the donors would be free to choose, creating a market-like interplay between donors and programs, supply and demand'.[23]

Creating money to pay for aid seems like the perfect solution. But the basic problem is that it puts too much emphasis on the volume of aid as the key to development rather than the conditions and implementation of aid. Soros cites favourably the United Nations report authored by former Mexican President Ernesto Zedillo that calls for an increase of $50 billion in aid. Soros has fallen victim to the same myth that also ensnared Robert McNamara: that poverty can be solved by throwing money at it. The paradigm within which aid programmes operate is a far greater determinant of success, and this is absent from Soros's proposal, except for mention about a greater role of civil society organizations in aid delivery.

The Soros proposal, moreover, does not solve one of the key problems with the Bretton Woods system, which is the stranglehold on decision-making by the rich countries. The donors of SDRs – meaning the OECD countries – would still be the ones to decide which programmes or projects are worth supporting. As in the case of the World Development Authority proposed by the Meltzer Commission, the massive power imbalance that is at the heart of the Bretton Woods system of multilateral aid remains. Indeed, with no developing country representation assured either on the proposed board or among the funders' consortium, the outcomes could be worse under this 'market-like system' than under the present system.

When it comes to the IMF, Soros's critique of the institution follows the now familiar lines: the Fund pushed the capital markets of the Asian economies before they were prepared for it, thus creating the conditions for the Asian financial crisis; and when the crisis did hit, the Fund promoted pro-cyclical policies, such as tight budgets and high interest rates, that worsened the crisis. Soros says that he partly agrees with the conservative critique that the IMF's past interventions created 'moral hazard', but he says that this was to a great degree inevitable to attract private capital to the developing world since without some extra-market incentives, capital would not have flowed there.[24]

Soros's defence of the Fund as necessary to attract capital to the developing world suffers on two counts. First, given the conditions of limited profitability in the metropolitan economies in the early 1990s, foreign capital had no choice but to migrate to areas that were regarded as offering better opportunities profit-wise; in other words, it is likely that they would have done this whether these countries had IMF programmes or not. The example of Malaysia, Singapore, Hong Kong, China and Taiwan – all of which either had no IMF programmes or had inconsequential ones – underlines this.

Second, the sort of capital that was encouraged to enter developing country capital markets by the possibility of an IMF rescue in the event things soured was speculative capital, which was mainly interested in high rate of return, quick turnaround investments such as the stockmarket or real estate. This is not the kind of capital that contributes to development. The dynamics of foreign direct investment, which involves a strategic commitment to the economy, is not determined by IMF guarantees.

The importance he attaches to the Fund as a mechanism of getting capital to flow to the developing world is what makes Soros support strengthening the IMF despite what he acknowledges as its poor record in the developing world. Some reforms that Soros seeks are viable. 'Bailing in' lenders instead of bailing them out – that is, having them participate with financing a rescue programme and agreeing to take losses in the process – is one. Establishing an international bankruptcy mechanism that would protect the debtor and allow an orderly process of both economic recovery for the debtor and asset recovery for the creditor is another, though Soros again subverts his own proposal by tying this initiative to the IMF.[25]

However, establishing a contingency credit line (CCL) that countries with 'good policies' can tap into before a crisis begins is unsound, for two reasons which have already been pointed out by other critics and of which Soros is aware: first, few countries would dare take advantage of CCLs for fear of alarming investors that a crisis is impending and thus create conditions for a stampede; second, the IMF's ability to distinguish good from bad policies.

Thus we are back to the fundamental problem. The Fund is saddled with a paradigm that puts a premium on macroeconomic stability, legal and political conditions that promote the interests of foreign capital, and the unrestricted functioning of the market. This paradigm, coupled with the United States Treasury's propensity to use the IMF to use the Fund to advance US economic and corporate interests, is at the heart of the Fund's succession of failures in the developing world. Giving the Fund more power like offering CCLs and managing an international bankrupt regime is tantamount to rewarding failure. Like the Meltzer Commission, Soros begins by criticizing the Fund for wrong policies but ends up believing that it 'needs to play a larger rather than a lesser role ...'[26] Like the Meltzer Commission, Soros fails to follow his analysis to its logical conclusion: abolition.

Notes

1. Commission on Global Governance, p. 161.

2. Ibid.

3. Ibid., pp. 280–1.

4. International Financial Institutions Advisory Commission Report to the US House of Representatives, March 8, 2000. The Meltzer Commission included both liberals and conservatives, though it was dominated by conservatives. The most prominent liberal member was Harvard economics professor Jeffrey Sachs.

5. Ibid.

6. Ibid.

7. See Focus on the Global South, *Profiting from Poverty: The ADB, the Private Sector, and Development in Asia* (Bangkok: Focus on the Global South, 2001; and *Profiting from Poverty: The ADB in Asia* (Bangkok: Focus on the Global South, 2000).

8. Among the writings that might be said to belong broadly to this viewpoint are the following: UNCTAD, 'The Management and Prevention of Financial Crises', *Trade and Development Report 1998*; Dani Rodrik, 'The Global Fix', *New Republic*, November 2, 1998 (downloaded from the Internet); John Eatwell and Lance Taylor, 'International Capital Markets and the Future of Economic Policy', *CEPA Working Paper No. 9*, Center for Economic Policy Analysis (CEPA) (New York: New School for Social Research, 1998; Roy Culpeper, 'New Economic Architecture: Getting the Right Specs', remarks at the Conference, 'The Asian Crisis and Beyond: Prospects for the 21st Century', Carleton University, Ottawa, January 29, 1999.

9. The reserve requirement was brought down to 0 per cent in October 1998, allegedly because speculative inflows had dropped considerably owing to the Asian financial crisis.

10. See, for instance, Culpeper, 'New Economic Architecture ...'

11. Eatwell and Taylor, p. 14.

12. Joseph Stiglitz, 'An Agenda for the G-7', proposals presented at the 2020 Visions Conference, Dunsmuir Lodge, Victoria, Canada, August 29–31, 2001.

13. Ibid.

14. Ann Florini, 'A Scenario for Running the World', paper prepared for the 2020 Visions Conference, Dunsmuir Lodge, Victoria, Canada, August 29–31, 2001.

15. Rodrik, 'The Global Fix ... '

16. Ibid.

17. George Soros, *On Globalization* (New York: Public Affairs, 2002), p. 32.

18. Ibid., p. 40.

19. Ibid., p. 38.

20. Ibid., p. 103.

21. Personal communication, Prague, September 23, 2000; Budapest, October 18, 2001.

22. Personal communication, Budapest, October 18, 2001.

23. Soros, pp. 78–9.

24. Ibid., p. 115.

25. Ibid., pp. 132–47.

26. Ibid., p. 115.

SEVEN
The Alternative: Deglobalization

The crisis that is wrenching the current system of global economic governance is a systemic one. It is not one that can be addressed by mere adjustments within the system, for these would be merely marginal in their impact or they might merely postpone a bigger crisis. To borrow the insights of Thomas Kuhn's classic *Structure of Scientific Revolutions*, when a paradigm is in crisis, there are two responses. One is that followed by the adherents of the old Ptolemaic paradigm, which was to make more and more complicated adjustments to their system of explanation until it became too complex and virtually useless in promoting scientific advance. This is the approach taken by most of the proposals for reform discussed above.

The other path was that taken by the partisans of the new Copernican system, which was to break away completely from the old paradigm and work within the parameters of the competing paradigm, which could not only accommodate dissonant data in a far more simple fashion but also point to new exciting problems.[1] This is the direction proposed in this book.

In contrast to science, however, breaking with the past is a far more complicated affair when it comes to global economic governance. In social change, new systems cannot really be effectively constructed without weakening the hold of old systems, which do not take fundamental challenges to their hegemony lightly. A crisis of legitimacy is critical in weakening current structures, but it is not enough. A vision of a new world may be entrancing, but it will remain a vision without a hard strategy

for realizing it, and part of that strategy is the deliberate dismantling of the old.

Thus a strategy of *deconstruction* must necessarily proceed along-
side one of *reconstruction*.

Deconstruction

The big anti-corporate globalization demonstrations of the last
few years have been right in bringing up the strategic demand of
dismantling the WTO and the Bretton Woods institutions. Advancing this demand and getting more and more people behind it
has been central in creating the crisis of legitimacy of these
institutions.

Tactically, however, it would be important to try to bring
coalitions together on more broadly acceptable goals, the achievement of which can nevertheless have a big impact in terms of
drastically reducing the power of these institutions or effectively
neutering them. In the case of the IMF, for instance, a demand
that has potential to unite a broad front of people is that of
converting it into a research agency with no policy powers but
one tasked with the job of monitoring global capital and exchange
rate movements – in other words turning it into an advisory and
research institution along the lines of the Organisation for Economic Co-operation and Development (OECD).

In the case of the World Bank, uniting with the demand to
end its loan-making capacity and devolving its grant activities to
appropriate regional institutions marked by participatory processes
(which would eliminate the Asian Development and other
existing regional development banks as alternatives) could serve
as a point of unity for diverse political forces and be a major step
to effectively disempowering it. These initiatives could be co-
ordinated with campaigns to boycott World Bank bonds, deny
new appropriations for the International Development Association
(IDA), and oppose calls for quota increases for the IMF. Unlike
the Soros approach, the thrust of this multi-dimensional effort

would be not one of reforming but drastically shrinking the power and jurisdiction of the Bretton Woods institutions.

Given its centrality and unique characteristics as a global institution, however, it is the WTO that must be the main target of the deconstruction enterprise. It is especially critical in the period leading up the Fifth Ministerial Meeting of this most powerful of the multilateral agencies of global governance.

The strategy of the deconstruction enterprise must respond to the needs of the moment in the struggle against corporate-driven globalization. This can be derived only by identifying the strategic objective, accurately assessing the global context or conjuncture, and elaborating an effective strategy and tactical repertoire that responds to the particularities of the conjuncture.

For the movement against corporate-driven globalization, it seems fairly clear that the strategic goal must be halting or reversing WTO-mandated liberalization in trade and trade-related areas. The context or 'conjuncture' is characterized by a fragile victory on the part of the free trade globalizers at the Fourth Ministerial at Doha, where they bludgeoned developing countries into agreeing to a limited round of trade talks for more liberalization on agriculture, services and industrial tariffs. The conjuncture is marked by the globalizers' effort to build momentum so as to have the Fifth Ministerial in Mexico launch negotiations for liberalization in the so-called trade-related areas of investment, competition policy, government procurement and trade facilitation. *Their aim is to have the Fifth Ministerial expand the limited set of negotiations they extracted at Doha into a comprehensive round of negotiations that would rival the Uruguay Round.*

This expansion of the free trade mandate and the expansion of the power and jurisdiction of the WTO, which is now the most powerful multilateral instrument of the global corporations, is a mortal threat to development, social justice and equity, and the environment. And it is the goal that we must thwart at all costs, for we might as well kiss goodbye to sustainable development, social justice, equity and the environment if the big trading powers and their corporate elites have their way and launch another global round for liberalization during the WTO's Fifth Ministerial Assembly in Mexico in 2003.

Given the strategic goal of stopping and reversing trade liberalization, the campaign objective on which the movement against corporate-driven globalization must focus its efforts and energies is simple and stark: derailing the drive for free trade at the Fifth Ministerial, which will serve as the key global mechanism for advancing free trade.

As noted earlier, the free trade partisan C. Fred Bergsten, head of the Institute of International Economics (IIE), has compared free trade and the WTO to a bicycle: they collapse if they do not move forward. Which is why Seattle was such a mortal threat to the WTO and why the globalizers were so determined to extract a mandate for liberalization at Doha. Had they failed at Doha, the likely prospect was not simply a stalemate but a retreat from free trade. For the movement against corporate-driven globalization, derailing the Fifth Ministerial or preventing agreement on the launching of a new comprehensive round would mean not only fighting the WTO and free trade to a standstill. It would mean creating momentum for a rollback of free trade and a reduction of the power of the WTO. This is well understood by, among others, *The Economist*, which warned its corporate readers that 'globalization is reversible'.

If derailing the drive for free trade at the 5th Ministerial is indeed the goal, then the main tactical focus of the strategy becomes clear: *consensus decision-making is the Achilles' heel of the WTO, and it is the emergence of consensus that we must prevent at all costs from emerging.*

Before the Fifth Ministerial, the anti-corporate globalization movement must focus its energy on ensuring that countries do not come into agreement in any of the areas now being negotiated or about to be negotiated, that is, agriculture, services and industrial tariffs; and at the Ministerial itself, preventing any consensus from emerging on negotiating the new issues of government procurement, competition policy, investment and trade facilitation. The aim must be, as in Seattle, to have the delegates go to the Ministerial with a 'heavily bracketed' declaration – that is, one where there is no consensus on the key issues – and at the Ministerial itself, to prevent consensus via last-minute horse-trading. *As in Seattle, the end goal must be to have the Ministerial end in disagreement and lack of consensus.*

If the goal is unhinging the game plan for greater free trade at the Fifth Ministerial, then the anti-corporate globalization movement has its work cut out for it. We must unfold a multi-pronged strategy whose components must include:

- unravelling the alliance between US Trade Representative Robert Zoellick and EU Trade Commissioner Pascal Lamy by exacerbating the US–EU conflict on Europe's agricultural subsidies, the Bush administration's failure to obtain unrestricted fast-track authority to negotiate from the USA's Senate, Washington's imposition of protective tariffs on steel and its resurgent trade unilateralism, and the US export of hormone-treated beef and genetically modified organisms (GMOs);
- intensifying our efforts to assist developing country delegations in Geneva to master the WTO process and formulate effective strategies to block the emergence of consensus on the areas prioritized by the trading powers and reassert the priority of implementation issues;
- working with national movements, such as peasant movements for food sovereignty in the South and citizens' movements in the North, to build massive pressure on their governments not to agree to further liberalization in agriculture, services, and other areas being negotiated;
- skilfully co-ordinating global protests, mass street action at the site of the ministerial, and lobby work in Geneva to create a global critical mass with momentum in the lead-up to the ministerial.

The task is immense and we have so little time. But we have

no choice. The trading powers and the WTO learned from Seattle, and they brought the bicycle of the WTO back on its wheels in Doha. Likewise, we must learn from Doha so that we can wrestle the bicycle back to the ground in Mexico. And among the key lessons we need to absorb is that our coalition must have a co-ordinated strategy that brings our work on many different fronts, levels and dimensions to bear on one goal: unhinging the drive for free trade at the Fifth Ministerial.

Deglobalizing in a Pluralist World

Hand in hand with the deconstruction campaign must unfold the reconstruction process or the enterprise to set up an alternative system of global governance.

There is a crying need for an alternative system of global governance. The idea is floating around that thinking about an alternative system of global governance is a task that for the most part is still in a primeval state. In fact, many or most of the basic or broad principles for an alternative order have already been articulated, *and it is really a question of specifying these broad principles to concrete societies in ways that respect the diversity of societies.*

Work on alternatives has been a collective past and present effort, one to which many in the North and South have contributed. The key points of this collective effort might be synthesized as a double movement of 'deglobalization' of the national economy and the construction of a 'pluralist system of global economic governance'.

The context for the discussion of deglobalization is the increasing evidence not only of the poverty, inequality and stagnation that have accompanied the spread of globalized systems of production but also of their unsustainability and fragility. The International Forum on Globalization (IFG) points out, for instance, that

the average plate of food eaten in western industrial food-importing nations is likely to have travelled 2,000 miles from source to plate. Each one of those miles contributes to the environmental and social crises of our times. Shortening the distance between producer and consumer has to be one of the crucial reform goals of any transition away from industrial agriculture.'[2]

Or as Barry Lynn has asserted, so much industrial production has been outsourced to a few areas such as Taiwan, that, had the earthquake of September 21, 1999 experienced by that island been 'a few tenths of a point stronger, or centered a few miles closer to the vital Hsinchu industrial park, great swaths of the world economy could have been paralyzed for months'.[3]

What is deglobalization? While the following proposal is derived principally from the experience of societies in the South, it has relevance as well to the economies of the North.

Deglobalization is not about withdrawing from the international economy. It is about reorienting economies from the emphasis on production for export to production for the local market.

- drawing most of a country's financial resources for development from within rather than becoming dependent on foreign investment and foreign financial markets;
- carrying out the long-postponed measures of income redistribution and land redistribution to create a vibrant internal market that would be the anchor of the economy and create the financial resources for investment;
- de-emphasizing growth and maximizing equity in order radically to reduce environmental disequilibrium;
- not leaving strategic economic decisions to the market but making them subject to democratic choice;
- subjecting the private sector and the state to constant monitoring by civil society;
- creating a new production and exchange complex that includes community co-operatives, private enterprises and state enterprises, and excludes TNCs;

- enshrining the principle of subsidiarity in economic life by encouraging production of goods to take place at the community and national level if it can be done at reasonable cost in order to preserve community.

This is, moreover, about an approach that consciously subordinates the logic of the market, the pursuit of cost efficiency, to the values of security, equity and social solidarity. This is, to use the language of the great social democratic scholar Karl Polanyi, about re-embedding the economy in society, rather than having society driven by the economy.[4]

True, efficiency in the narrow terms of constant reduction of unit costs may well suffer, but what will be gained – or perhaps the most appropriate term is regained – are the conditions for the development of integrity, solidarity, community, greater and more democracy, and sustainability.

It is these principles that today drive many bold enterprises that have achieved some success, mainly at a local, community level. As Kevin Danaher of Global Exchange has pointed out, the list includes fair trade arrangements between Southern farmers and Northern consumers in coffee and other commodities, microcredit schemes such as the Grameen Bank, community currency systems delinking exchange from global and national monetary systems and linking it to local production and consumption, participatory budgeting as in Porto Alegre, and sustainable eco-communities such as Gaviotas in Colombia.[5]

The reigning god, however, is a jealous one that will not take lightly challenges to its hegemony. Even the smallest experiment must either be smashed or emasculated, as the imperious Bank of Thailand did when it told several villages in the Kud Chum district in Thailand's Northeast region to abandon their local currency system. Peaceful co-existence between different systems is, unfortunately, ultimately not an option.

Thus deglobalization or the re-empowerment of the local and national, however, can only succeed if it takes place within an alternative system of global economic governance. The emergence of such a system is, of course, dependent on greatly reducing the power of the Western corporations that are the main drivers of globalization and the political and military hegemony of the states – particularly the United States – that protect them. But even as we devise strategies to erode the power of the corporations and the dominant states, we need to envision and already lay the groundwork for an alternative system of global economic governance.

What are the contours of such a world economic order? The answer to this is suggested by our critique of the Bretton Woods-cum-WTO system as a monolithic system of universal rules imposed by highly centralized institutions to further the interests of corporations – and, in particular, US corporations. To try to supplant this with another centralized global system of rules and institutions, although these may be premised on different principles, is likely to reproduce the same Jurassic trap that ensnared organizations as different as IBM, the IMF and the Soviet state, and this is the inability to tolerate and profit from diversity. Incidentally, the idea that the need for one central set of global rules is unquestionable and that the challenge is to replace the neoliberal rules with social democratic ones is a remnant of a techno-optimist variant of Marxism that infuses both the Social Democratic and Leninist visions of the world, producing what Indian author Arundhati Roy calls the predilection for 'gigantism'.

Today's need is not another centralized global institution but the deconcentration and decentralization of institutional power and the creation of a pluralistic system of institutions and organizations interacting with one another, guided by broad and flexible agreements and understandings.

This is not something completely new. For it was under such a more pluralistic system of global economic governance, where hegemonic power was still far from institutionalized in a set of all-encompassing and powerful multilateral organizations and institutions, that a number of Latin American and Asian countries were able to achieve a modicum of industrial development in the period from 1950 to 1970. It was under such a pluralistic system, under a General Agreement on Tariffs and Trade (GATT) that was limited in its power, flexible and more sympathetic to the special status of developing countries, that the East and South-east Asian countries were able to become newly industrializing countries through activist state trade and industrial policies that departed significantly from the free market biases enshrined in the WTO.

Of course, economic relations among countries prior to the attempt to institutionalize one global free market system beginning in the early 1980s were not ideal, nor were the Third World economies that resulted ideal. They failed to address a number of needs illuminated by recent advances in feminist, ecological and post-post-development economics. What is simply being pointed out is that the pre-1994 situation underlines the fact that the alternative to an economic Pax Romana built around the World Bank–IMF–WTO system is not a Hobbesian state of nature. The reality of international relations in a world marked by a multiplicity of international and regional institutions that check one another is a far cry from the propaganda image of a 'nasty' and 'brutish' world the partisans of the WTO evoked in order to stampede the developing country governments to ratify the WTO in 1994.

Of course, the threat of unilateral action by the powerful is ever present in such a system, but it is one that even the most powerful hesitate to take for fear of its consequences on their legitimacy as well as the reaction it would provoke in the form of opposing coalitions.

In other words, what developing countries and international civil society should aim at is not to reform the TNC-driven WTO and Bretton Woods institutions, but, through a combination of passive and active measures, to either a) decommission them; b) neuter them (e.g., converting the IMF into a pure research institution monitoring exchange rates of global capital flows); or c) radically reduce their powers and turn them into just another set of actors co-existing with and being checked by other international organizations, agreements and regional groupings. This strategy would include strengthening diverse actors and institutions such as UNCTAD, multilateral environmental agreements, the International Labor Organization and regional economic blocs.

Regional economic blocs in the South would be important actors in this process of economic devolution. But they would have to be developed beyond their current manifestations in the European Union, Mercosur in Latin America and ASEAN (Association of Southeast Asian Nations) in Southeast Asia.

A key aspect of 'strengthening', of course, is making sure these formations evolve in a people-oriented direction and cease to remain regional elite projects. Trade efficiency in neoclassical economic terms should be supplanted as the key criterion of union by 'capacity building'. That is, trade would have to be reoriented from its present dynamics of locking communities and countries into a division of labour that diminishes their capabilities in the name of 'comparative advantage' and 'interdependence'. It must be transformed into a process that enhances the capacities of communities, that ensures that initial cleavages that develop owing to initial division-of-labour agreements do not congeal into permanent cleavages, and which has mechanisms, including income, capital, and technology-sharing arrangements that prevent exploitative arrangements from developing among trading communities.

Needless to say, the formation of such regional blocs must actively involve not only government and business but also NGOs and people's organizations. Indeed, the agenda of people-oriented sustainable development can succeed only if it is evolved democratically rather than imposed from above by regional elites, as was the case with the European Union, Mercosur and ASEAN. Regional integration has increasingly become an essential condition for national development, but it can be effective only if it is carried out as a project of economic union from below.

Many of the elements of a pluralist system of global economic governance already exist, but there are undoubtedly others that

need to be established. Here the emphasis must be on the formation of international and regional institutions that would be
dedicated to creating and protecting the space for devolving the
greater part of production, trade and economic decision-making
to the regional, national and community level. One such institution is the establishment of an effective international organization
for the preservation and strengthening of the economies of the
hundreds of thousands of indigenous economies throughout the
world.

Indeed, a central role of international organizations in a world
where toleration of diversity is a central principle of economic
organization would be, as the British philosopher John Gray puts
it, 'to express and protect local and national cultures by embody-
ing and sheltering their distinctive practices'.[5]

More space, more flexibility, more compromise – these should
be the goals of the Southern agenda and the international civil
society effort to build a new system of global economic governance. It is in such a more fluid, less structured, more pluralistic
world, with multiple checks and balances, that the nations and
communities of the South – and the North – will be able to
carve out the space to develop based on their values, their
rhythms, and the strategies of their choice.

Notes

1. See Thomas Kuhn, *The Structure of Scientific Revolutions* (Chicago:
University of Chicago Press, 1971).

2. John Cavanagh et al., 'Alternatives to Economic Globalization', International Forum on Globalization, San Francisco.

3. Barry Lynn, 'Unmade in America: The True Cost of a Global Assembly Line', *Harper's*, June 2002, p. 36.

4. See Karl Polanyi, *The Great Transformation* (Boston: Beacon, 1957).

5. Speech at the University of Montana, Missoula, Montana, June 16,
2002.

6. John Gray, *Enlightenment's Wake* (London: Routledge, 1995), p. 181.

Selected Readings

An excellent critique of corporate-driven globalization that is informed by a profound sociological, philosophical and historical perspective is John Gray's *False Dawn* (New York: New Press, 1999).

One of the best collections of critical essays on economic globalization is Edward Goldsmith and Jerry Mander, *The Case against the Global Economy* (London: Earthscan, 2001).

Naomi Klein's *No Logo* (London: HarperCollins, 2001) and David Korten's *When Corporations Rule the World* (Bloomfield, CT: Kumarian Press, 2001) are two of the most insightful works on the dynamics of transnational corporation in the age of globalization.

The crisis of profitability and overproduction that forms the backdrop of the unending stream of corporate corruption in Wall Street is brilliantly analysed by Robert Brenner in two works: 'The Economics of Global Turbulence', *New Left Review* 229 (May–June 1998) (whole issue) and *The Bubble and the Boom* (London: Verso, 2002).

Different dimensions of global instability in the age of capitalist globalization driven by the financial sector are analysed in Walden Bello, Nicola Bullard and Kamal Malhotra, eds, *Global Finance* (London: Zed Books, 2000).

Globalization and its Discontents (New York: W.W. Norton, 2002) by Joseph Stiglitz, former chief economist of the World Bank, is definitely worth reading. However, all the key points made by Stiglitz were made, more convincingly, 28 years ago by Cheryl Payer in *The Debt Trap* (New York: Monthly Review Press, 1974). Similarly, little written today by the growing ranks of ex-Bretton

Woods staffers can match the classical critiques of the World Bank: Frances Moore Lappé and Joe Collins, *Food First* (San Francisco: Food First, 1975); Robin Broad, *Unequal Alliance* (Berkeley: University of California Press, 1985); Bruce Rich, *Mortgaging the Earth* (New York: 1993); and Susan George and Fabrizio Sabelli, *Faith and Credit* (London: Penguin, 1995).

A useful resource for campaigners on the IMF is American Friends Service Committee, *An IMF Primer: Selected Resources on the International Monetary Fund* (Philadelphia: American Friends Service Committee, 2002).

Different dimensions of world trade and the World Trade Organization are analysed in *Why Reform of the WTO is the Wrong Agenda* (Bangkok: Focus on the Global South, 2000); Debi Barker and Jerry Mander, *Invisible Government: The WTO – Global Governance for the New Millenium* (San Francisco: International Forum on Globalization, 1999); Aileen Kwa, *Power Politics in the WTO: Developing Country Perspectives on Decision-making Processes in Trade Negotiations* (http://focusweb.org, 2002); Oxfam International, *Rigged Rules and Double Standards* (London: Oxfam International, 2002); and Mark Curtis, *Trade for Life: Making Trade Work for Poor People* (London: Christian Aid, 2001).

The perspectives of Southern thinkers and activists – Vandana Shiva, Anuradha Mittal, Sarah Larrain, Oronto Douglas, Martin Khor and Dot Keet – on various aspects of globalization are presented in Sarah Anderson, ed., *Views from the South* (San Francisco: International Forum on Globalization, 1999). Also expounding a Third World viewpoint are Martin Khor, *Rethinking Globalization* (London: Zed Books, 2001) and Walden Bello, *The Future in the Balance* (Oakland, CA: Food First, 2001).

A excellent complement to Noam Chomsky's various books on Washington's imperial ways is Chalmers Johnson, *Blowback: The Costs and Consequences of American Empire* (New York: Henry Holt and Company, 2000). Provocative and profound analyses of September 11 and its consequences are brought together in two publications: Katrina Van den Heuvel, ed., *A Just Response:* The

Nation *on Terrorism, Democracy, and September 11, 2001* (New York: Nation Books, 2002); and Roger Burbach and Ben Clarke, eds, *September 11 and the US War: Beyond the Curtain of Smoke* (San Francisco: City Lights, 2002). Michael Mann provides an insightful analysis of the relationship of September 11 to globalization in 'Globalization after September 11', *New Left Review*, No. 12, Second Series (November–December 2001), pp. 51–72.

The diversity and dynamism of the global movement against corporate-driven globalization are captured in Robin Broad, ed., *Global Backlash* (Lanham, MD: Rowman and Littlefield, 2002). Interesting and useful proposals for transforming the global economy are presented in Dani Rodrik, *The Global Governance of Trade as if Development Really Mattered* (New York: United Nations Development Programme, 2001), John Cavanagh, Jerry Mander et al., *Alternatives to Economic Globalization* (San Francisco: International Forum on Globalization, 2002) and Colin Hines, *Localization: A Global Manifesto* (London: Earthscan, 2000).

Selected Organizations
Monitoring Multilateral Organizations
and Global Governance Issues

50 Years Is Enough Network

3628 12th St. NE, Washington, DC 20017, USA
www.50years.org; tel. 1 202 463 2265

ActionAid

Hamlyn House, Macdonald Road, London N19 5PG,
Great Britain
www.actionaid.org; tel. 44 (0)20 7561 7561

American Friends Service Committee

International Programs, 1501 Cherry Street, Philadelphia,
Pennsylvania 19102–1479, USA
www.afsc.org/location.htm; tel. 1 215 241 7000

Attac

Contacts in 32 countries can be accessed at www.attac.org

Bank Information Center

733 15th St. NW # 1126, Washington, DC 20005, USA
www.bicusa.org; tel. 1 202 737 7752

Bread for the World

50 F St. NW #500, Washington, DC 20001, USA
www.bread.org; tel. 1 202 639 9400

Bretton Woods Project

c/o ActionAid, Hamlyn House, Macdonald Road, London
N19 5PG, Great Britain
Awood@gn.apc.org; tel. 44 (0)20 7561 7545/47

Catholic Fund for Overseas Development (CAFOD)

Romero Close, Stockwell Road, London SW9 9TY, Great Britain
www.cafod.org.uk; tel. 44 171 733 7900

Center for Concern Rethinking the Bretton Woods Project

1225 Otis St. NE, Washington, DC 20017, USA
www.coc.org; tel. 1 202 635 2757

Center for Economic and Policy Research

1621 Connecticut Ave. NW, Suite 500, Washington, DC 20009, USA
www.cepr.net; tel. 1 202 265 3263

Christian Aid

35 Lower Marsh, Waterloo Road, London SE1 7RL, Great Britain
www.christian-aid.org.uk; tel. 44 (0)20 7620 4444

Citizens' Network on Essential Services (CNES)

(formerly Globalization Challenge Initiative)
7000-B Carroll Ave. #101
Takoma Park, MD 20912, USA
www.ServicesForAll.org; tel. 1 301 270 1000

Development GAP

925 15th St. NW, 4th Flr
Washington, DC 20005, USA
www.developmentgap.org; tel. 1 202 898 1566

Essential Action

P.O. Box 19405, Washington, DC 20036, USA
www.essentialaction.org; tel. 1 202 387 8030

Equipo Pueblo

Mexico City, Mexico
Pueblo@laneta.apc.org; tel. 525 539 0015

Focus on the Global South

Chulalongkorn University Social Research Institute, Chulalongkorn
University, Bangkok 10330, Thailand
www.focusweb.org; tel. 66 2 218 7363

Food First

398 60th St., Oakland, CA 94618, Oakland, California, USA
www.foodfirst.org; tel. 1 510 654 4400

Freedom from Debt Coalition (Philippines)

www.fdc.org.ph; tel. 63 2 921 1985

Friends of the Earth International

PO Box 19199, gd Amsterdam, Netherlands
www.foei.org; tel. 31 20 622 1369

Global Exchange

2017 Mission St. #303, San Francisco, CA 94110, USA
www.globalexchange.org; tel. 1 415 255 7296

Infid (International NGO Forum on Indonesian Development

Jalan Mampang Prapatan XI No. 23 12790, Indonesia
www.nusa.or.id; tel. 62 21 791 96721

Institute for Agriculture and Trade Policy

2105 First Avenue South, Minneapolis, MN 55404, USA
www.iatp.org; tel. 1 612 870 0453

Institute for Policy Studies

733 15th St. NW, Suite 1020, Washington, DC 20005
www.ips–dc.org; tel. 1 202 344 9382

International Center for Trade and Sustainable Development

13 chemin des Anémones, 1219 Geneva, Switzerland
www.ictsd.org; tel. 41 22 917 8492

International Development Exchange

827 Valencia St. #101, San Francisco, CA 94110-1736, USA
www.idex.org; tel. 1 415 824 8384

International Forum on Globalization

1009 Gen. Kennedy Ave, #2, San Francisco, CA, USA
www.ifg.org; tel. 1 415 561 7650

New Economics Foundation

Cinnamon House, 6-8 Cole Street, London, SE1 4YH, United
Kingdom
www.neweconomics.org; tel. 44 (0)20 7089 2800

Oxfam International Advocacy Office

1112 16th St. NW #600, Washington, DC 20036
www.oxfaminternational.org; tel. 1 202 496 1170

South Centre

Chemin du Champ d'Anier 17, Case postale 228, 1211 Geneva 19,
Switzerland
www.southcentre.org; tel. 41 22 791 8050

Third World Network

228 MacAlister Road 10400, Penang, Malaysia
www.twnside.org.sg; tel. 60 4 226 6728

Third World Network/Africa

PO Box 8604, Accra-North, Ghana
Isodec@mantse.ncs.com.gh; tel. 233 21 301064

Transnational Institute

Paulus Potterstraat 20, 1071 DA Amsterdam, The Netherlands
www.tni.org; tel. 31 20 662 6608

United Nations Conference on Trade and Development Division on Globalization and Development

Palais des Nations, CH-1211, Geneva 10, Switzerland
Yilmaz Akyuz, OIC
Yilmaz.akyuz@unctad.org; tel. 41 22 907 5841

United Nations Development Program

Human Development Report Office
336 East 45th St., New York, NY 10017, USA
www.undp.org/undp/hdro; tel. 1 212 906 3600

Via Campesina

Operational Secretariat, Rafael Alegria, Consejo Coordinador de
Organizaciones, Campesinas de Honduras, LOCOCH, Barrio La
Plazuela, Calle Real de la P.C., Casa No. 934 Apdo, CP 3628,
Tegucigalpa, Honduras
www.virtualsask.com/via/

WALHI

Jalan Mampoang Prapatan IV; Jalan K No. 37 12790, Indonesia
Walhi@pacific.net.id; tel. 62 21 794 1672

World Development Movement

25 Beehive Place, London SW9 7QR, United Kingdom
wdm@wdm.org.uk; tel. 44 20 7274 8232

World Social Forum

Rua General Jardim, 6608 Andar, Sala 81, Cep 01223-010, São Paulo,
Brazil
www.forumsocialmundial.org.br/; tel. 55 11 3258 4466

Index

Participating Organizations

Both ENDS: A service and advocacy organization that collaborates with environment and indigenous organizations, both in the South and in the North, with the aim of helping to create and sustain a vigilant and effective environmental movement.

Damrak 28-30, 1012 LJ Amsterdam, The Netherlands
Tel: +31 20 623 0823   Fax: +31 20 620 8049
E-mail: info@bothends.org
Website: www.bothends.org

Catholic Institute for International Relations (CIIR): CIIR aims to contribute to the eradication of poverty through a programme that combines advocacy at national and international level with community-based development.

Unit 3 Canonbury Yard, 190a New North Road,
London N1 7BJ, UK
Tel: +44 (0)20 7354 0883   Fax: +44 (0)20 7359 0017
E-mail: ciir@ciir.org
Website: www.ciir.org

Corner House: The Corner House is a UK-based research and solidarity group working on social and environmental justice issues in North and South.

PO Box 3137, Station Road, Sturminster Newton,
Dorset DT10 1YJ, UK
Tel: +44 (0)1258 473795   Fax: +44 (0)1258 473748
E-mail: cornerhouse@gn.apc.org
Website: www.cornerhouse.icaap.org

Council on International and Public Affairs (CIPA): CIPA is a human rights research, education and advocacy group, with a particular focus on economic and social rights in the USA and elsewhere around the world. Emphasis in recent years has been given to resistance to corporate domination.

777 United Nations Plaza, Suite 3C, New York, NY 10017, USA
Tel: +1 212 972 9877   Fax: +1 212 972 9878
E-mail: cipany@igc.org
Website: www.cipa-apex.org

Dag Hammarskjöld Foundation: The Dag Hammarskjöld Foundation, established in 1962, organizes seminars and workshops on social, economic and cultural issues facing developing countries, with a particular focus on alternative and innovative solutions. Results are published in its journal *Develpment Dialogue*.

> Övre Slottsgatan 2, 753 10 Uppsala, Sweden.
> Tel: +46 18 102772   Fax: +46 18 122072
> E-mail: secretariat@dhf.uu.se
> Website: www.dhf.uu.se

Development GAP: The Development Group for Alternative Policies is a non-profit development resource organization working with popular organizations in the South and their Northern partners in support of a development that is truly sustainable and that advances social justice.

> 927 15th Street, NW, 4th Floor, Washington, DC 20005, USA
> Tel: +1 202 898 1566   Fax: +1 202 898 1612
> E-mail: dgap@igc.org
> Website: www.developmentgap.org

Focus on the Global South: Focus is dedicated to regional and global policy analysis and advocacy work. It works to strengthen the capacity of organizations of the poor and marginalized people of the South and to better analyse and understand the impacts of the globalization process on their daily lives.

> c/o CUSRI, Chulalongkorn University, Bangkok 10330, Thailand
> Tel: +66 2 218 7363   Fax: +66 2 255 9976
> E-mail: Admin@focusweb.org
> Website: www.focusweb.org

Inter Pares: Inter Pares, a Canadian social justice organization, has been active since 1975 in building relationships with Third World development groups and providing support for community-based development programmes. Inter Pares is also involved in education and advocacy in Canada, promoting understanding about the causes and effects of, and solutions to, poverty.

> 58 rue Arthur Street, Ottawa, Ontario, K1R 7B9 Canada
> Tel: + 1 613 563 4801   Fax: + 1 613 594 4704

Public Interest Research Centre: PIRC is a research and campaigning group based in Delhi that seeks to serve the information needs of activists and organizations working on macro-economic issues concerning finance, trade and development.

142, Maitri Apartments, Plot No. 28, Patparganj, Delhi: 110092, India
Tel: + 91 11 2221081, 2432054   Fax: + 91 11 2224233
E-mail: kaval@nde.vsnl.net.in

Third World Network: TWN is an international network of groups and individuals involved in efforts to bring about a greater articulation of the needs and rights of peoples in the Third World; a fair distribution of the world's resources; and forms of development that are ecologically sustainable and fulfil human needs. Its international secretariat is based in Penang, Malaysia.

228 Macalister Road, 10400 Penang, Malaysia
Tel: +60 4 226 6159   Fax: +60 4 226 4505
E-mail: twnet@po.jaring.my
Website: www.twnside.org.sg

Third World Network–Africa: TWN–Africa is engaged in research and advocacy on economic, environmental and gender issues. In relation to its current particular interest in globalization and Africa, its work focuses on trade and investment, the extractive sectors and gender and economic reform.

2 Ollenu Street, East Legon, PO Box AN19452, Accra-North, Ghana.
Tel: +233 21 511189/503669/500419   Fax: +233 21 511188
E-mail: twnafrica@ghana.com

World Development Movement (WDM): The World Development Movement campaigns to tackle the causes of poverty and injustice. It is a democratic membership movement that works with partners in the South to cancel unpayable debt and break the ties of IMF conditionality, for fairer trade and investment rules, and for strong international rules on multinationals.

25 Beehive Place, London SW9 7QR, UK
Tel: +44 (0)20 7737 6215   Fax: +44 (0)20 7274 8232
E-mail: wdm@wdm.org.uk
Website: www.wdm.org.uk

The Global Issues Series

Roger Moody, *Digging the Dirt: The Modern World of Global Mining*

Peter Robbins, *The Commodities Disaster: What Can be Done?*

Kavaljit Singh, *The Myth of Globalization: Ten Questions Everyone Asks*

Keith Suter, *Curbing Corporate Power: How Can We Control Transnational Corporations?*

Nedd Willard, *The War on Drugs: Is This the Solution?*

For full details of this list and Zed's other subject and general catalogues, please write to: The Marketing Department, Zed Books, 7 Cynthia Street, London N1 9JF, UK or e-mail:

sales@zedbooks.demon.co.uk

Visit our website at: http://www.zedbooks.demon.co.uk

This book is also available in the following countries:

CARIBBEAN

Ian Randle Publishers, 11 Cunningham Avenue
Box 686, Kingston 6, Jamaica, W.I.
Tel: (876) 978 0745, 978 0739   Fax: 978 1158
e-mail: ianr@colis.com

EGYPT

MERIC (The Middle East Readers' Information Center)
2 Bahgat Ali Street, Tower D/Apt. 24 Zamalek, Cairo
Tel: 20 2 735 3818/736 3824   Fax: 20 2 736 9355

FIJI

University Book Centre, University of South Pacific, Suva
Tel: 679 313 900   Fax: 679 303 265

GHANA

EPP Book Services, PO Box TF 490, Trade Fair, Accra
Tel: 233 21 773087   Fax: 233 21 779099

MAURITIUS

Editions Le Printemps, 4 Club Road, Vacoas, Mauritius

MOZAMBIQUE

Sul Sensacoes, PO Box 2242, Maputo
Tel: 258 1 421974   Fax: 258 1 423414

NAMIBIA

Book Den, PO Box 3469, Shop 4, Frans Indongo Gardens,
Windhoek
Tel: 264 61 239976   Fax: 264 61 234248

NEPAL

Everest Media Services, GPO Box 5443, Dillibazar, Putalisadak
Chowk, Kathmandu
Tel: 977 1 416026   Fax: 977 1 250176

Papua New Guinea

Unisearch PNG Pty Ltd, Box 320, University, National Capital
District
Tel: 675 326 0130   Fax: 675 326 0127

Philippines

IBON Foundation, Inc., 3rd Floor SCC Bldg.,
4427 Int. Old Sta. Mesa, Manila, Philippines 1008
Tel: (632) 713-2729 / 713-2737   Fax: (632) 716-0108

Rwanda

Librairie Ikirezi, PO Box 443, Kigali
Tel/Fax: 250 71314

Tanzania

TEMA Publishing Co Ltd, PO Box 63115, Dar Es Salaam
Tel: 255 51 113608   Fax: 255 51 110472

Uganda

Aristoc Booklex Ltd, PO Box 5130, Kampala Road, Diamond
Trust Building, Kampala
Tel/Fax: 256 41 254867

Zambia

UNZA Press, PO Box 32379, Lusaka
Tel: 260 1 290409   Fax: 260 1 253952

Zimbabwe

Weaver Press, PO Box A1922, Avondale, Harare
Tel: 263 4 308330   Fax: 263 4 339645